Jesus

AND

The Gospel of Q

✿ THE LOCHLAINN SEABROOK COLLECTION ✿

Enlightening Books, Educational Films, & Entertaining Music for the Whole Family!

JESUS

AND THE GOSPEL OF Q

Christ's Pre-Christian Teachings
As Recorded In The New Testament

Lochlainn Seabrook

SEA RAVEN PRESS, NASHVILLE, TENNESSEE, USA

JESUS AND THE GOSPEL OF Q

Published by
Sea Raven Press, PO Box 1484, Spring Hill, Tennessee 37174-1484 USA
www.searavenpress.com • searavenpress@nii.net

First Sea Raven Press Edition: May 2014
ISBN: 978-0-9913779-1-6
Library of Congress Catalog Number: 2014938352

Jesus and the Gospel of Q: Christ's Pre-Christian Teachings as Recorded in the
New Testament, by Lochlainn Seabrook. Includes endnotes, index, and
bibliographical references.

Front and back cover design and art, book design, layout, and interior art by Lochlainn Seabrook
Typography: Sea Raven Press Book Design
All images, graphic design, graphic art, and illustrations © Lochlainn Seabrook
Cover image: "The Resurrection," Carl Heinrich Bloch, 1873, © Lochlainn Seabrook

The paper used in this book is acid-free and lignin-free. It has been certified by the Sustainable Forestry
Initiative and the Forest Stewardship Council and meets all ANSI standards for archival quality paper.

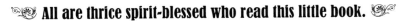 **All are thrice spirit-blessed who read this little book.**

PRINTED & MANUFACTURED IN OCCUPIED TENNESSEE, FORMER CONFEDERATE STATES OF AMERICA

Dedication

To the courageous 19th-Century theological explorers who uncovered and identified Q and its sequential layers, establishing its importance to both Bible scholarship and the Christian faith.

Epigraph

Because it reveals the authentic Jesus
while exposing the false one invented by
the mainstream Church, The Gospel of Q
is the most important document we
currently have in our quest to fully
understand our Lord, His true and
original "Gospel of the Kingdom," His
first followers, and primitive Christianity.

Lochlainn Seabrook, 2014

CONTENTS

SECTION 1
Q¹, Q², Q³, & Qᶜ ACCORDING TO LUKE

SECTION 2
THE GOSPEL OF Q ACCORDING TO MARK & MATTHEW

Notes to the Reader

✠ All canonical Bible passages are from the King James Version (KJV), unless otherwise noted. As a result, my readings and interpretations may differ from those found in other versions. Because of this, I highly recommend the use of the KJV in combination with *Jesus and the Gospel of Q*.

✠ Though many of the Bible's books are pseudepigraphical (that is, their authors are unknown or, more often, are falsely attributed), for simplicity's sake when discussing them I use the authors ascribed by Christian tradition.

✠ All italics within Bible passages are mine (used for emphasis), while bracketed words within Bible passages contain my comments and corrections.

✠ Unlike many other Q researchers, I have maintained the respectful tradition of capitalizing pronouns associated with Jesus, e.g., He, His, Him, Himself, etc.

✠ Unlike the traditional Q scriptural numbering system which, for instance, lists Q 6:20-23 (i.e., Luke 6:20-23) as "QS8," I supply each Q passage with its own individual number, just as the Bible does. Thus in this book, for example, Q 6:20 in Luke is given the listing Q1LK2 (meaning Q^1, as recorded in Luke, scripture 2), Q 6:21 is given the listing Q1LK3, Q 6:22 is listed as Q1LK3, and so on. Note that my Q scriptural numbering system is not related to the numbering systems of the Synoptic Gospels or to any of those created by other Q researchers and scholars.

✠ I list the Q scriptures in the exact order they appear in the Synoptic Gospels. Thus, because Matthew, Mark, and Luke have at times rearranged the original order of Q, some passages may appear out of context, not only within a particular canonical Gospel, but in comparison to the other two Synoptic Gospels as well.

✠ While I have included Q^1, Q^2, $Q^{3,}$ and Q^C as found in Luke, as well as all of the vestiges of Q that remain in Mark, I have included only Q^1 and Q^C of Matthew. This is because I consider Luke's Q to be more precise than Matthew's. As for my inclusion of Q^1 (but not Q^2 or Q^3) in Matthew, this is due to the extreme significance of Q's first layer, which I believe cannot be overstated.

✠ It should be understood that the passages of Q, as they have been culled herein from Matthew, Mark, and Luke, may not (and almost certainly do not) always represent Q's original wording, but only as they have come down to us filtered through the Synoptics. The Evangelists, who were not authors but rather editors, copyists, and mythologists, no doubt felt free to alter the wording of Q to fit their own needs (which explains the many discrepancies in wording, meaning, usage, and order of Q passages scattered throughout Matthew, Mark, and Luke). Since the original Q document has yet to be found, the original wording of Q also remains unknown.

✠ There is no universal agreement on exactly which New Testament scriptures belong to Q and which do not. I myself have my own ideas as to which passages were once part of Q. As a result, my versions of Q differ from those reconstructed by others—some who include far more New Testament material than I do (which, as Kloppenborg states, has created "expanded" editions of Q that are both overly cumbersome and of limited value).[1] Thus I have tended toward a conservative approach to scriptural membership in Q. While it will be found that most modern day reconstructions of Q vary (sometimes widely), all, in one way or another, convey and retain much of the original intent, tenor, vigor, and import of this priceless document.

✠ I am a Christian and this is a Christian book (though one that can be read and enjoyed by individuals of any faith). Yet, it is not associated with any specific Christian denomination, sect, faction, church, society, schism, community, organization, or cult. What it *is* associated with are what I consider to be some of the original and authentic teachings of Jesus as they appear in the Gospel of Q as preserved in the New Testament.

✠ Though as a Q researcher who sometimes disagrees with their findings, beliefs, and opinions, I am indebted to the many scholars and researchers (both living and deceased) who have preceded me, and who have done the yeoman's work in researching Q. All Christians should be grateful for their erudition, courage, and perseverance in advancing our understanding of the authentic Jesus, as well as the development of the New Testament and the so-called "early Church."

Dei Sit In Omni Homine

ABBREVIATIONS

TRADITIONAL DESIGNATIONS
Q: *Quelle*, German for "source."

Q^1: The first or oldest layer of Q.
Q^2: The second or middle layer of Q.
Q^3: The third or most recent layer of Q.

Q^{MT}: Q as recorded in the Gospel of Matthew.
Q^{MK}: Q as recorded in the Gospel of Mark.
Q^{LK}: Q as recorded in the Gospel of Luke.

SEABROOK DESIGNATIONS
Q1MT: Q^1 layer as found in the Gospel of Matthew.
Q2MT: Q^2 layer as found in the Gospel of Matthew.
Q3MT: Q^3 layer as found in the Gospel of Matthew.
QCMT: Complete Q as recorded in the Gospel of Matthew.

Q1MK: Q^1 layer as found in the Gospel of Mark.
Q2MK: Q^2 layer as found in the Gospel of Mark.
Q3MK: Q^3 layer as found in the Gospel of Mark.
QCMK: Complete Q as recorded in the Gospel of Mark.

Q1LK: Q^1 layer as found in the Gospel of Luke.
Q2LK: Q^2 layer as found in the Gospel of Luke.
Q3LK: Q^3 layer as found in the Gospel of Luke.
QCLK: Complete Q as recorded in the Gospel of Luke.

Q or QC: The complete text of Q, which includes all of Q^1, Q^2, and Q^3.

PREFACE
Why I Wrote This Book

C onservative theologians reject Q while asserting the divinity of Jesus. Liberal theologians, on the other hand, assert the reality of Q while rejecting the divinity of Jesus. I belong to neither of these schools, for I assert and accept the reality of both Q and Jesus' divine nature.

For me the Gospel of Q is not, as many claim, a hypothetical construct, invented by anti-Christian intellectuals to strip the title "Messiah" from the Lord and diminish Christianity in the eyes of the world. Q is a real, living, breathing, document, filled with what I consider to be some of the most spiritually powerful, dynamic, and transformational doctrines ever uttered by Man or Woman.

These doctrines were grouped together in what Jesus called, "The Gospel of the Kingdom,"[2] a series of often startling notions that are meant, like the Buddhist Koan, to shock the system in order to alter and raise one's consciousness. The goal? The psycho-spiritual attainment of what Hindus call "samadhi," what Dr. Carl G. Jung called "individuation," what Christian mystics call "Christ Consciousness,"[3] what Paul knew as "the mind of Christ,"[4] and what Jesus referred to more mystically as "the Kingdom of God (or Heaven)."[5]

This "kingdom" is not a material kingdom and has nothing to do with the Church, Christianity, or even religion;[6] rather it is a spiritual one pertaining exclusively to the individual.[7] It is a state of mind or consciousness which our Lord located uncategorically not outside of us, but *inside* of us. As He Himself put it:

> Neither shall they say, Lo here! or, lo there! for, behold, *the kingdom of God is within you.*[8]

As I have discussed the Kingdom Within at great length in my other works,[9] I need not delve deeply into this topic here, other than to repeat the all-important words of the Master:

> Seek ye first the kingdom of God, and his righteousness; and all these things shall be added unto you.[10]

Tragically, following His crucifixion, Jesus' followers quickly forgot these poignant phrases, and the emphasis went from Jesus' teachings to Jesus Himself, after which His "Gospel of the Kingdom" was summarily renamed "The Gospel of Jesus Christ." Jesus' insistence that we concentrate on the Father rather than on Himself[11] was completely disregarded and even suppressed. It was during this nefarious process that *the focus went from the message to the messenger*, and we Western Christians have been laboring under the fabricated delusions of organized Christianity ever since!

Along with this sweeping and devastating change (away from the authority of Jesus and the Spirit to the authority of the Church and the Priesthood), our Lord's authentic words have become ever more remote, as the Bible has now gone through hundreds of translations worldwide—most which are merely thinly disguised attempts by their translators to promote their own personal religious ideology. As a supporter of the First Amendment of the U.S. Constitution, I have no inherent problem with this. However, for those of us who are interested in the genuine teachings of the Lamb of God, this is a wholly unsatisfactory situation.

Yet there is a solution, however imperfect.

It is my opinion that we can scarcely get closer to Jesus' true words than what is to be found in The Gospel of Q, and it is from out of this sentiment that I wrote *Jesus and the Gospel of Q*. Not as merely another long and detailed academic dissection of Q (a type of book, by the way, that I happen to enjoy and which certainly has its place). But rather one in which everyday Christians can share and revel in the Living Word of God, which is just as vibrant and active today as it was 2,000 years ago.

To this end, and to counter the ongoing deteriorating trend away from Jesus' true Gospel, in this book I have used what is still Christendom's favorite Bible translation: the 17th-Century King James Version or KJV.

I am well aware of its many thousands of translational errors (some number them over 36,000).[12] Despite this, I still consider the KJV to be nearer the truth in most instances than the majority of modern Bible translations. And since I am the only modern day Q researcher who uses the KJV (most consider the KJV "inferior," and so like to offer their own "fresh" translations), *Jesus and the Gospel of Q: Christ's Pre-Christian Teachings as Recorded in the New Testament*, stands alone as a unique and important work that can benefit both ordinary Christians and religious scholars.

It is my prayer that this small humble book helps to revive and preserve the original thoughts and teachings of our Lord, and that in doing so it will spread the hope and inspiration embedded in His universal message, the *true* "Good News" of the New Testament: The Christ is in the Father, we are in The Christ, The Christ is in us, and all three are one.[13] This makes us immortal *and* possessed of the same Divine Nature[14] and powers as Jesus, just as He Himself declared.[15]

Lochlainn Seabrook
God-written, May Day 2014
Nashville, Tennessee, USA
In Nobis Regnat Christos ("Within Us Reigns Christ")

INTRODUCTION
A Brief Discussion of the Gospel of Q

DEFINING Q

What is The Gospel of Q? Awareness of what would come to be called Q first began in the early 1800s with various theologians, such as Herbert Marsh, Friedrich Schleiermacher, and Christian Weisse, who began searching for a hypothetical source for the matching scriptures in Matthew and Luke but that are not found overtly in Mark.

By the mid to late 1800s other scholars, like Heinrich J. Holtzmann, Adolf Harnack, Paul Wernle, Julius Wellhausen, Bernhard Weiss, and his son Johannes Weiss (who coined the letter-title "Q"),[16] joined in the quest, which grew in interest and intensity into the 1900s. The 20th Century marked a period of ever increasingly sophisticated studies by such individuals as Burnett H. Streeter, Pierson Parker, James M. Robinson, Helmut Koester, John S. Kloppenborg, and Burton L. Mack.

Despite this learned roster, the search to understand Q continues unabated to this day, with no one theory answering every question and dilemma posed by this elusive document.

Q derives its name from the German word *quelle*, meaning "source," for Q contains the source material for a large percentage of the Synoptic Gospels: canonical Matthew and Luke, and to a smaller degree Mark. (As of yet there is no evidence that the Gnostically influenced John used Q or even knew of it,[17] though this does not mean that his Gospel does not also contain some of Jesus' original words.)[18] Thus, parts of the Synoptic Gospels are comprised of precious remnants of what are (or what are close to) the Lord's actual statements—as opposed to the fabricated "quotes" artificially inserted by the Roman Church hundreds of years later.[19]

Though the original Q document is no longer extant, additional evidence for its one time existence may be found in the works of the 2nd-Century Bishop Papias of Hierapolis,[20] Saint Paul,[21] Clement of Rome,[22] and perhaps Luke.[23]

Q IS PRE-CHRISTIAN, THE CHRISTIAN CHURCH IS POST-JESUS

As paleographic evidence shows, The Gospel of Q, of course, predates the four canonical Gospels, with the earliest "layer" (known as Q[1]) probably being written down from the Lord's oral teachings as early as the 30s (shortly after His death),[24] Q[2] being composed sometime in the 40s and 50s, and Q[3] written as late as the year 75.[25]

Fascinatingly *and* revealingly, Q[1] does not mention or delve into the personal life of Jesus, His birth, baptism, messiahship,[26] the Last Supper, the Agony, His trial, crucifixion, transfiguration, resurrection, or ascension. In fact, "all references to the Passion are absent from Q."[27] Q's earliest layer also contains no apocalyptic warnings, no martyrological dogma, no complex theodicies, no salvific creeds, no named apostles, and no rules or instructions on how to organize and maintain the community of Q (which authored Q)—or any future type of "church" for that matter[28]—proving, just as our Lord Himself said, that He never intended to found a new religion.[29]

Q[1] does not even mention the phrase "son of God," so integral to the foundation of modern institutionalized Christianity. This is, in part, because

> the compilation in Q was intended solely for the Christian community and was addressed to those who did not require the assurance that their Teacher was also the Son of God.[30]

Instead, throughout Q[1] Jesus refers to Himself as the "son of Man,"[31] an everyday ancient Aramaic expression meaning simply a "human being."[32] (We will note here that the expression "Son of God" is used only in Q[3], the one layer of Q that is completely fictitious, an invented section compiled by individuals who were unfamiliar with the real Jesus—as portrayed in Q[1]—but who were obviously very well acquainted with the standard Judeo-Pagan hero and savior myths of the time.)

Likewise, the kerygma (the "apostolic proclamation of salvation through Jesus Christ"),[33] the very basis of the modern day mainstream Christian Church, is itself entirely absent from Q[1]. In fact, because "Q has no interest in Christological apologetics,"[34] the kerygma appears nowhere in any layer of Q, which means that Christianity as we know it today was nonexistent during and shortly after Jesus' life. Q[1] is, in other words, a pre-Christian document, making orthodox Christianity a post-Jesus institution.

As one would expect from the earliest followers of the Jewish Master whom they respectfully called "Rabbi" (that is, "Teacher"),[35] Q centers not on Jesus, but on Jesus' *teachings*, most which pertain to the mystical "Kingdom Within."[36] In the words of Harnack, the author [of Q] is simply concerned with the commandments of our Lord, and aims at giving a description of His message, in which description He appears to be influenced by no special and particular bias.[37]

It should be emphasized here that neither Jesus or His first followers were "Christians," and never thought of themselves as such—which is why this word does not appear anywhere in either Q or the four canonical Gospels.[38]

Other Jesuine teachings from The Gospel of Q that are found in the New Testament are the pre-Christian forms of the Lord's Prayer,[39] the Pagans' Golden Rule, some of the Beatitudes, and many of His parables (most which, again, center on the all-important Christological concept of the Kingdom of God, or what I term "the Realm of Divine Mind").[40]

THE CREATION & EVOLUTION OF Q

Q probably began life during Jesus' ministry, perhaps during the first year, A.D. 30, as a collection of the earliest shared oral traditions surrounding His elementary Aramaic teachings, which He Himself called *The Gospel of the Kingdom.*[41]

Shortly after His death these sayings must have been gathered together into a written document, perhaps by the mid 30s. Today this first edition or "layer" is known as Q^1 to distinguish it from subsequent additions to the text. Q^1 contains blunt, razor-sharp, Zen-like aphorisms that are known as Jesus' "wisdom sayings" (in Greek, *logoi sophon*),[42] and so it is often referred to by theologians as the layer containing His "sapiential instructions." While Jesus Himself referred to these expressions as "sayings,"[43] as did three of the Gospelers,[44] as a Christian I believe they represent part of the Lord's true *teachings*, which is why I have used this particular word in the subtitle of this book instead of "sayings," the traditional word.

Sometime later, probably between the 40s and 50s, a second layer was appended to Q^1. This strata, one containing apocalyptic or prophetic material, became known as Q^2.

Finally, perhaps around the year 75, the third and last layer was added. A brief grouping of mythological passages, heavily laden with legendary Near Eastern Judeo-Pagan savior and hero elements, it was called Q^3.

I refer to the combined text of all three layers as QC, for "Q Complete"; that is, the complete Gospel of Q as it has been retained in the

New Testament.

THE PRESENT GOSPEL OF Q IS NOT TRULY "COMPLETE"

In reality, as it now stands, Q cannot be considered "complete" in the true sense of the word, since much of the Master's authentic Gospel was lost even before the canonical Gospels were compiled. One scholar, Anthony M. Honoré, has estimated that at least 40 percent of Q was not preserved in the New Testament.[45] John and Luke both commented on the fact that there is omitted (or missing) Jesuine material,[46] as did Paul.[47]

We must also consider the fact that countless literary treasures related to Jesus and His teachings have been lost over the last 2,000 years due to the burning and suppression of wrongly called "heretical" pre-Christian (e.g., Essene) and Christian (e.g., Gnostic) texts, as well as through innumerable modern retranslations of the Bible (diabolical processes that, unfortunately, persist into the present day).

MY VIEWS OF THE GOSPEL OF Q

Tens of thousands of pages of exhaustive and often brilliant Q studies have been published since the early 1800s, and heated debate continues to swirl around this extraordinary sayings collection of Jesus, which we now know as The Book of Q or, as I prefer, The Gospel of Q. Deliberations range from when it was composed and by whom, to where it originated and why it was written, to what should be included and what should be excluded[48]—with some scholars even arguing against Q's existence.[49]

I have my own opinions of Q, some which diverge sharply from "accepted" mainstream ideas and theories.

Q WAS A REAL DOCUMENT

I believe that Q was a real document (a physical scroll), a pre-Christian, pre-New Testament, pre-clerical, pre-canonical written record of Jesus' sayings and teachings, which long predated the formation of the ecclesiastical Church (i.e., Roman Catholicism) and the religion that would later be called "Christianity" (authentic history shows that both, like the New Testament, are essentially syncretistic products of the 4th Century).

There is no other logical explanation for the fact that Matthew and Luke have matching passages that are identical or nearly identical in wording.[50] For lack of a better title then, what we now call "Q" must be the *Grundschrift* (that is, the "basic writing," or first primitive Gospel) behind the

Synoptic Gospels of the New Testament. As such, it must have once existed, first orally, later in physical form as a written document.

Q IS A GOSPEL

Though today an ancient writing is only considered a "gospel" if it fits in with the structural, stylistic, poetic, organizational, grammatical, theological, compositional, qualitative, narrative, and thematic makeup and characteristics of the four canonical Gospels, this criteria is far too narrow in my opinion.

I believe that since the word gospel literally means a "good tale," or more generally the "good news" (in this case, about The Christ and the Kingdom Within), any early literary work that encompasses this type of message should be considered a gospel. Q perfectly fits this description. Thus it is a part of, or is itself, the first actual Gospel of Jesus—a sizeable remnant, as mentioned, of what He called "The Gospel of the Kingdom."[51]

Q IS NOT TRULY "LOST"

While many consider Q to be "lost," I consider it to be found, for much of it has been uncovered in Matthew and Luke, and too a lesser extent in Mark. Though understandably most Q scholars will never be entirely satisfied until the original Q document (if it, or a copy of it, still exists) is discovered (and this is always a possibility), we can take solace in the fact that some 60 percent of it has been preserved in the New Testament.

It is worth noting that while early orthodox Church authorities claimed that there were only three "lost" Gospels (those of Philip, Matthias, and Thomas),[52] there were actually many dozens (perhaps even hundreds) of Gospels penned by Gnostic Christians, Pagan Christians, and Jewish Christians between the 1st and 4th Centuries, most of which have disappeared. Fortunately some of these truly "lost" Gospels have been rediscovered, including The Gospel of Thomas, The Gospel of Philip, The Gospel of Mary, and The Secret Gospel of Mark, to name just a few.[53]

Q WAS ORIGINALLY WRITTEN IN ARAMAIC IN PALESTINE

I believe that Q was composed in Palestine,[54] and that it first spread in Aramaic, the language Jesus spoke.[55] It was later translated into Greek—though this translation was probably derived from oral sayings rather than directly from the first Aramaic Q scroll.[56]

Q'S PROVENANCE IS UNKNOWABLE

Currently Q is missing a title, an incipit (opening words), and a colophon (information about authorship, location, date, etc.). It is also only discernable by meticulously extracting it from documents (the Synoptic Gospels) that are themselves copies of material that has been thoroughly rewritten, redacted, and reworked over many centuries by people, many with, it must be said, unchristian motives, and who had no interest whatsoever in either history or historical accuracy. Hence, at this time it is not possible to know the precise identity of Q's "author(s)," his/her exact purpose for compiling the material contained within Q, or where and when Q was composed.

Q IS THE TRUE LIVING TESTAMENT OF THE GOSPEL OF JESUS

For Christians like myself (I would be more accurately called a follower of Jesus, or a Jesuist), Q is not just a mere collection of anonymous "sayings" steeped in a common Near Eastern sayings tradition, as many liberal theologians maintain. Nor do I see it as just a "hypothetical construct," as some conservative theologians hold.

For me Q is a historical spiritual compendium of the authentic teachings of our Lord, which along with The Gospel of Thomas, represents our best currently known sources of Jesus' *earliest* thoughts, statements, and beliefs. Since Q predates even Thomas, this makes Q the most ancient written record of our Lord;[57] it is the veritable testimony of the first so-called "Christians";[58] it is the literary Holy Grail that contains Jesus' most pure and unadulterated doctrines. I agree, in other words, with Harnack, who in 1908 wrote that

> this compilation of sayings . . . alone affords us a really exact and profound conception of the teaching of Jesus . . . [because it] is free from bias, apologetic or otherwise . . .[59]

Q HAS NO NARRATIVE OR CHRONOLOGY

Unlike the canonical Gospels, Q lacks a cohesive narrative as well as a coherent structure of time. Instead its compiler grouped Q's material "catechetically according to its subjects."[60] Fortunately for posterity, this "unimaginative" approach allows us a glimpse of the real Jesus, stripped of those later fictitious scriptural accumulations that have served only to conceal rather than reveal both His true character and the true meaning behind His words.

Q EVOLVED OVER TIME

Like the Bible itself, Q developed in "successive steps" or "separate stages," as German Bible scholar Adolf Jülicher phrased it over 100 years ago,[61] while around the same period Harnack correctly hypothesized the evolutionary stages of Q as "Q^1, Q^2, Q^3, Q^4, etc."[62]

Q WAS CREATED IN THREE STAGES

Q naturally divides into three levels or layers, graduating from a primitive, simple, and realistic form to a more sophisticated, ornate, and mythological one, all assembled over a period of about 45 years (circa A.D. 30-75).

The first layer of Q, called Q^1, contains much of Jesus' original and undefiled teachings, which both He and the canonical Gospelers referred to as "The Gospel of the Kingdom (of God or Heaven)."[63] In my estimation at least 95 to 99 percent of this specific wisdom material is genuine, direct from the mouth of the Lord.

When Jesus' followers came to realize that the promised imminent Parousia (Second Coming) would not occur in their lifetimes (as both Jesus and Paul had said it would—if we are to take their words *literally*),[64] they began adding fictitious apocalyptic material to Q^1, mixing it with some of the Master's authentic words in an attempt to both assuage their disappointment and to dilute the failed Parousian predictions. Thus Q^2, as this second layer is called, was probably a result of the need of the Jesus (Q) community to fortify its own personal beliefs and political agendas, as the sociopolitical environment of the Graeco-Roman world changed, often violently, around them. In my opinion only 50 percent (or less) of the wording in Q^2 is from Jesus.

Q^3, the folkloric layer, was wholly fabricated by Jesus followers, most who had never known or met Him. Though some of this late material may have been based on elements of authentic Jesuine material, much of it is clearly Judeo-Pagan in origin, part of the great savior mythos of the ancient Near Eastern and European *weltanschauung*.[65] Because of this, my theory is that almost none of Q^3 comes from Jesus (even though some of this material *may* have reflected His beliefs).

JESUS & THE WISDOM-GODDESS SOPHIA

I believe that Q (particularly Q^1) portrays Jesus precisely as He was viewed and understood by His pre-Christian followers, the Jesus people (or Q community, as they are also sometimes known): not as the much anticipated supernatural Jewish Messiah, but as an earthly though celebrated human teacher; like Chrishna, Buddha, and Zoroaster before Him, a literal bearer of Divine Wisdom—which in ancient times was personified as a female deity (known, for example, in Greece as the goddess Sophia,[66] in Rome as Sapientia, in India as Sarasvati, and in Judaism as Chokmah). Hence Q^1 and Q^2 refer to Jesus not as "the Son of God" but as "the Sophia of God."[67]

THE SYNOPTIC PROBLEM

I believe that there is no one ideal solution to the riddle of the "Synoptic Question" or "Synoptic Problem" (that is, how the first three Gospels were created). For example, the origins of at least one/fifth of Matthew and one/third of Luke are still unknown.[68] Nonetheless, it is clear that all three of the Synoptic Gospelers used multiple sources, including Q.

MARK THE GREAT MYTHOGRAPHER USED Q

The great mythographer, emender, and recensionist Mark, who purposefully set out to alter and formulate Christian tradition,[69] certainly used Q,[70] though this fact is not generally recognized because he reinterpreted, remolded, and rewrote it, while borrowing numerous standard elements, archetypes, motifs, legends, symbols, and other trappings from pre-Christian Judaism and Paganism.

Most notable among these is his appropriation of the universally popular human sacrificial Mystery Play or Passion Play and its lead mock-king character, the "Royal Savior" of mankind. In this annually dramatized public theatrical event, the savior's life story was comprised of a group of archetypal themes, such as a virgin birth, temptation by the Devil, selection of twelve apostles, performance of miracles, parabolic teachings, the preaching of a radical but salvific philosophy, his transfiguration, resistance by orthodox religionists, sacramental meal of "flesh" and "blood," and finally the betrayal of his disloyal associates, and his suffering, trial, crucifixion, wounding on the cross (or tree), and resurrection after three days.[71]

Since the motivation behind the Passion Play of the mock-king was to promote agricultural fertility, it was designed as a solar allegory of the Sun's passage through the twelve star-signs of the Zodiac[72]—which is why the savior was always "born" at the Winter Solstice and "killed" and "raised up" at the Spring Equinox. The interested student will find this standard astro-agrarian drama attached to scores of pre-Christian saviors, including Osiris, Attis, Mithras, Chrishna, Buddha, Dionysus, Horus, Baal, Tammuz,

Marduk, Balder, Odin, Quetzalcoatl, Adonis, the Son of Righteousness, and Joshua, among countless others.[73]

What was Mark's purpose for tapping into this rich vein of mythological Judeo-Pagan savior material?

It suited his personal goal: the mythic portrayal of Jesus as the supernatural only begotten Son of God,[74] the long awaited Christ or Messiah,[75] superior to all other saviors before Him. It is because of Mark's indiscriminate, credulous, messy, patchwork-quilt method of "writing" (that is, borrowing, plagiarizing, refashioning, and "improving" the works of others) that Harnack wrote of this particular Gospel:

> . . . page by page the student is reduced to despair by the inconsistencies, the discrepancies, and the incredibilities of the narrative. . . . [For it is in Saint Mark that we find] an almost complete inability to distinguish between what is primary or secondary, between what is trustworthy or questionable, an apologetic which grasps at all within its reach, to which everything is welcome and right.[76]

MATTHEW THE GREAT REDACTIONIST USED Q

I believe that along with portions of Mark,[77] Matthew also relied heavily on Q. Though unlike Mark he retained much of what is to me Q's most important and fascinating aspect: Q^1. (Needless to say, I do not agree with the hoary theory that Matthew authored Q.)

LUKE THE GREAT COMPILER USED Q

Along with Mark, Luke also used Q (perhaps a different version),[78] but in a way that presents Q in a more orderly and understandable form than Matthew. Among most scholars (though not all) this has made Luke the gold standard as a Q reference.[79] I agree with this assessment, which is why I devote the first half of this book to Q^1, Q^2, Q^3, and QC as these layers appear in Luke: Luke best preserves Q as we have come to know it today.

Q'S DISAPPEARANCE & THE GOSPEL OF THOMAS

Toward the end of the 1st Century A.D., Q began to gradually disappear due to its absorption into subsequent writings,[80] such as the Synoptic Gospels and The Gospel of Thomas, another "sayings gospel" (some of whose sibylline doctrines can be found in the writings of early Christian mystics).[81] At least 35 percent of Q can be found in Thomas, while some

60 percent of Thomas derives specifically from Q^1.[82] This means that Thomas, written (50s-60s?) shortly after Q^1 and Q^2, could itself be a version of Q, or even Q itself.[83] Of Q's final disappearance Harnack writes:

> We cannot tell how long this compilation remained in existence. Its traces in St. Clement of Rome and in writers after his time are not certain. It found its grave in the gospels of St. Matthew and St. Luke, and probably elsewhere in some apocryphal gospels. St. Mark alone could not have supplanted it; but the narrative type of gospel, which was created by the second evangelist and which answered to the needs of catechetical apologetics, no longer allowed the separate existence of a compilation of sayings. The final blow to the independent existence of Q was dealt when it was incorporated in the gospels of St. Luke and St. Matthew. In St. Luke it exists, split up and dispersed throughout the gospel in subservience to the historical narrative; in St. Matthew it was treated in [a] more conservative spirit, though in some important passages it has suffered more from revision and shows clearer traces of the particular bias of the evangelist. In most skilful fashion—often only by means of an accent or by an arrangement of the context which seems quite insignificant—the first evangelist has made this compilation of discourses subservient to his own special interest in the Christian community and its organisation, while St. Luke, who has much more frequently altered the wording of his source, has nevertheless kept so closely to it in essential points that its original character is more clearly perceived in his reproduction.[84]

UNCOVERING Q IN THE SYNOPTICS

The "complete" 240 or so scriptures of The Gospel of Q, as found in the New Testament, can today be reconstructed from a study of the matching material found in Matthew and Luke, and more difficultly in Mark. The latter problem is due, as mentioned, to the fact that Mark ignored much of Q^1 while overhauling and remodeling most of Q^2 and Q^3, transforming Q as a whole into something almost unrecognizable.[85]

SOME Q PASSAGES WERE NOT UTTERED BY JESUS

Based on a close exegetical study of the development and evolution of the books of the New Testament (which proves that it must now be seen as largely a product of the 4th-Century Roman Church), it is clear that not every word attributed to Jesus in either Q or the Synoptic Gospels was actually said by Him.

WHY Q IS MISSING SOME OF JESUS' TEACHINGS
On the other hand, many things that Jesus actually said and taught are missing from Q. This may be because this material was lost; or perhaps the compilers simply chose to disregard it. In some cases, however, this could be due to the fact that His followers did not understand His more mystical doctrines, and so they intentionally neglected to add them to Q.

One example is Luke 17:20-21—two passages that many Q scholars regard as not being part of Q—in which the Master tells us that "the Kingdom of God is within you." The Q community was almost certainly expecting an *earthly* kingdom to manifest in "this generation."[86] When it did not arrive, confusion set in. They could not comprehend that Jesus' Kingdom was a *spiritual*, that is, a *psychological* one,[87] and so this particular teaching may not have been included in Q.[88]

How did it get into the present New Testament then?

If those who hold that Luke 17:20-21 was not part of Q are correct, then a posthumous follower who *did* understand the esoteric doctrine of the Inner Kingdom must have added it at a later date, sometime between the late 1st Century and the 4th Century.[89]

PAPIAS' REFERENCES TO Q
I believe, along with Schleiermacher,[90] that Papias' mention of a "Hebrew" version of Matthew is probably an ancient reference to an Aramaic version of Q, quite possibly the original,[91] and that Papias' statement that Mark copied down Jesus' *chreiai* (anecdotes) at the dictation of Peter may also be an allusion to Q. I quote these two passages by Papias here in full so that the reader may form his or her own judgement:

> [According to] the traditions of the Presbyter John, to which referring those that are desirous of learning them, we shall now subjoin to the extracts from him, already given, a tradition which he sets forth concerning Mark, who wrote the gospel in the following words: "And John the Presbyter also said this, Mark being the interpreter of Peter, whatsoever he recorded he wrote with great accuracy but not however, in the order in which it was spoken or done by our Lord, for he neither heard nor followed our Lord, but as before said, he was in company with Peter, who gave him such instruction as was necessary, but not to give a history of our Lord's discourses: wherefore Mark has not erred in any thing,

by writing some things as he has recorded them; for he was carefully attentive to one thing, not to pass by any thing that he heard, or to state any thing falsely in these accounts." Such is the account of Papias, respecting Mark. Of Matthew he has stated as follows: "Matthew composed his history in the Hebrew dialect, and every one translated it as he was able."[92]

THE Q EXPERIENCE

The best way to get what I call the full "Q experience" is to read Section One of *Jesus and the Gospel of Q* in chronological order, starting with Chapter One and ending with Chapter Four. This will allow you to see firsthand the manner in which The Gospel of Q was created and built up over time.

A perfect analogy would be to imagine a small house that was built by Jesus in the year 30 (Q^1). Then around the year 50, some twenty years after His death, a new second floor was added by some of His intimate friends (Q^2). Finally, around the year 75, two generations after Jesus' passing, a new wing was added by people who had never known or even met Him (Q^3). For the next several centuries, subsequent groups continued to add to the home until the first three layers disappeared entirely, subsumed into the new and ever growing framework (the four canonical Gospels and the other 23 books of the New Testament).

Continuing with our analogy, as each new addition was appended to the "home" Jesus built, it receded further and further from the original architectural design He had intended, until the final product (modern translations of the New Testament) looked nothing like it. To put this in context, we are now examining this ancient complex from a distance of 2,000 years, all without the benefit of having the blueprint (Q^1) that Jesus originally built from. To overcome this obstacle, the original structure (Q) has had to be reconstructed based on a detailed study of the new "additions" (Synoptic Gospels) appended by His followers hundreds of years after the fact. This is The Gospel of Q as we know and study it today.

WHY Q^1 IS A MOST INVALUABLE DOCUMENT

One of the most worthy aspects of The Gospel of Q is its oldest layer, Q^1, written, in my opinion, at least one or two generations before the earliest canonical Gospel, Mark. Through Q^1 we can see how the first followers of Jesus actually viewed Him, in the era before He was Paganized, apotheosized, and mythologized by Mark,[93] and subsequently by Emperor Constantine and the Roman Church.[94]

From even a casual reading of Q[1], it is patently obvious that the Q community (the original followers of Jesus) saw Him not as a god, messiah, savior, or even The Christ, but as an enlightened teacher, amazing physician, and extraordinary prophet. For true believers today this does not mean that He was *not* the Savior, the Only Begotten Son, however, nor does it necessarily call into question His divinity and ministry. It only indicates that the first so-called "Church" did not view Jesus in this way, and that His deification came only after His death.[95]

THE GOD-MAKING OF JESUS

And indeed, this turns out to be historically true: the orthodox Church did not formally declare Jesus a Savior-God until the year 325, at the Council of Nicaea,[96] while He was not officially accepted as part divine and part human until the year 451, at the Council of Chalcedon.[97] The Holy Cross—not a Christian symbol, but a universal one dating from the prehistoric period—was not even adopted by the Church until the 7th Century, and it did not become authorized for official use until the 9th Century.[98] Likewise, the Church did not permit Jesus' mother, the Virgin Mary, to be called *Theotokos* (the "God-bearer") until the year 431,[99] her bodily Assumption was not formulated until the 6th Century,[100] and the doctrine of the Immaculate Conception was not officially upheld until the year 1853.[101]

The earliest Christian letters corroborate these facts. The Epistle of James, for example, the oldest document in the New Testament (written about the year 35),[102] only refers to Jesus twice, makes no mention of His miraculous virgin birth, His followers (the Disciples), the Twelve Apostles, the Last Supper, His redemptive death on the cross, His resurrection, or even the Christian faith. Indeed, the anti-Pauline author James describes true religion as nothing more than "visiting the fatherless and widows in their affliction, and keeping yourself unspotted from the world."[103] (The absence of these fundamental Christian concepts here is all the more striking when we consider that James was Jesus' brother.)

Much of this could be said of Paul's letters as well, in particular Galatians, perhaps the second oldest document in the New Testament (written between the years 48 and 58).[104]

All of this illustrates that not only was the Church not founded by Jesus or even by His immediate followers (instead it was a product of politically motivated groups who gradually developed it over many centuries), but it also explains why there is no mention in Q^1 of the typical Pagan elements we are all so familiar with, such as His virgin mother, His step-father Joseph, the Star of Bethlehem, the manger, or the Three Wise Men. We have already noted that Q as a whole neglects to reference Jesus' Christhood, the Twelve Apostles, the Church, His arguments with the Pharisees, or even the Passion.[105] Let the reader think on these things.

HOW Q BENEFITS THE MODERN CHRISTIAN

Whether one chooses to literally believe in these late mythological Pagan components or not,[106] one thing is certain: lacking them, Q^1 is able to show us, more realistically than ever before, the genuine Jesus, the authentic mystical preacher of the pre-Christian era, one unencumbered by centuries of fictitious Jewish and Pagan accretions. How can this be so? One of our most sagacious Bible scholars answered the question this way. Q, he said, is "a compilation of discourses and sayings of our Lord, the arrangement of which has no reference to the Passion, with an horizon which is as good as absolutely bounded by Galilee, without any clearly discernible bias, whether apologetic, didactic, ecclesiastical, national, or anti-national."[107]

This then is Q's unique gift to us. And what a revelation it has disclosed!

The enlightened individual at the center of Q lived in a pre-Christian world influenced, not by encrusted exoteric Christian dogma and so-called ecclesiastical "tradition," but by the essentially esoteric Essenic and Gnostic spirituality that permeated the region at the time. And this is precisely how Jesus was perceived by those who knew Him best: His contemporary followers, the very authors of Q. In fact, vestiges of this view of Jesus, not as a deity, but rather as a highly illuminated man and a God-realized educator, seer, and doctor, remain scattered throughout the canonical New Testament. Study these passages and decide who and what Jesus was for yourself.[108]

But if Paul was correct, and I believe he was, in declaring that we are all anointed Christs, that The Christ indwells each and every one of us,[109] then Jesus was indeed a "wisdom teacher,"[110] the Gospel of Q is proved true, and the layer known as Q^1 is the most important Christian document ever written. As Harnack phrased it:

> No words of mine are needed to explain what this means for our knowledge of the history of our Lord.[111]

SECTION 1

Q^1, Q^2, Q^3, & Q^6
ACCORDING TO LUKE

1

Q¹ IN LUKE

THE FIRST LAYER OF THE GOSPEL OF Q
Q's Wisdom Teachings of Jesus in Luke

WRITTEN CIRCA A.D. 30S
96 VERSES FROM THE KING JAMES VERSION[112]

KEY FOR SEABROOK NUMBERING SYSTEM
IN BRIEF: "Q1LK1": Gospel of Q, layer, canonical Gospel, verse.
IN DETAIL: "Q1LK1" means Gospel of Q, layer 1, as found in
Gospel of Luke (KJV), first verse of layer 1.

Q1LK1 This is part of the true and original Gospel of the Kingdom as taught by Jesus.[113]

Q1LK2 Blessed be ye poor: for yours is the kingdom of God.[114]

Q1LK3 Blessed are ye that hunger now: for ye shall be filled. Blessed are ye that weep now: for ye shall laugh.[115]

Q1LK4 Blessed are ye, when men shall hate you, and when they shall separate you from their company, and shall reproach you, and cast out your name as evil, for the Son of man's sake.[116]

Q1LK5 For, behold, your reward is great in heaven.[117]

Q1LK6 But I say unto you which hear, Love your enemies, do good to them which hate you.[118]

Q1LK7 Bless them that curse you, and pray for them which despitefully use you.[119]

Q1LK8 And unto him that smiteth thee on the one cheek offer also the other; and him that taketh away thy cloke forbid not to take thy coat also.[120]

Q1LK9 Give to every man that asketh of thee; and of him that taketh away thy goods ask them not again.[121]

Q1LK10 And as ye would that men should do to you, do ye also to them likewise.[122]

Q1LK11 For if ye love them which love you, what thank have ye? for sinners also love those that love them.[123]

Q1LK12 And if ye do good to them which do good to you, what thank have ye? for sinners also do even the same.[124]

Q1LK13 And if ye lend to them of whom ye hope to receive, what thank have ye? for sinners also lend to sinners, to receive as much again.[125]

Q1LK14 But love ye your enemies, and do good, and lend, hoping for nothing again; and your reward shall be great, and ye shall be the children of the Highest: for he is kind unto the unthankful and to the evil.[126]

Q1LK15 Be ye therefore merciful, as your Father also is merciful.[127]

Q1LK16 Judge not, and ye shall not be judged: condemn not, and ye shall not be condemned: forgive, and ye shall be forgiven:[128]

Q1LK17 Give, and it shall be given unto you; good measure, pressed down, and shaken together, and running over, shall men give into your bosom. For with the same measure that ye mete withal it shall be measured to you again.[129]

Q1LK18 And he spake a parable unto them, Can the blind lead the blind? shall they not both fall into the ditch?[130]

Q1LK19 The disciple is not above his master: but every one that is perfect shall be as his master.[131]

Q1LK20 And why beholdest thou the mote that is in thy brother's eye, but perceivest not the beam that is in thine own eye?[132]

Q1LK21 Either how canst thou say to thy brother, Brother, let me pull out the mote that is in thine eye, when thou thyself beholdest not the beam that is in thine own eye? Thou hypocrite, cast out first the beam out of thine own eye, and then shalt thou see clearly to pull out the mote that is in thy brother's eye.[133]

Q1LK22 For a good tree bringeth not forth corrupt fruit; neither doth a corrupt tree bring forth good fruit.[134]

Q1LK23 For every tree is known by his own fruit. For of thorns men do not gather figs, nor of a bramble bush gather they grapes.[135]

Q1LK24 A good man out of the good treasure of his heart bringeth forth that which is good; and an evil man out of the evil treasure of his heart bringeth forth that which is evil: for of the abundance of the heart his mouth speaketh.[136]

Q1LK25 And why call ye me, Lord, Lord, and do not the things which I say?[137]

Q1LK26 Whosoever cometh to me, and heareth my sayings, and doeth them, I will shew you to whom he is like:[138]

Q1LK27 He is like a man which built an house, and digged deep, and laid the foundation on a rock: and when the flood arose, the stream beat vehemently upon that house, and could not shake it: for it was founded upon a rock.[139]

Q1LK28 But he that heareth, and doeth not, is like a man that without a foundation built an house upon the earth; against which the stream did beat vehemently, and immediately it fell; and the ruin of that house was great.[140]

Q1LK29 And it came to pass, that, as they went in the way, a certain man said unto him, Lord, I will follow thee whithersoever thou goest.[141]

Q1LK30 And Jesus said unto him, Foxes have holes, and birds of the air have nests; but the Son of man hath not where to lay his head.[142]

Q1LK31 And he said unto another, Follow me. But he said, Lord, suffer me first to go and bury my father.[143]

Q1LK32 Jesus said unto him, Let the dead bury their dead: but go thou and preach the kingdom of God.[144]

Q1LK33 And another also said, Lord, I will follow thee; but let me first go bid them farewell, which are at home at my house.[145]

Q1LK34 And Jesus said unto him, No man, having put his hand to the plough, and looking back, is fit for the kingdom of God.[146]

Q1LK35 [Speaking to His disciples, Jesus said:] The harvest truly is great, but the labourers are few: pray ye therefore the Lord of the harvest, that he would send forth labourers into his harvest.[147]

Q1LK36 Go your ways: behold, I send you forth as lambs among wolves.[148]

Q1LK37 Carry neither purse, nor scrip, nor shoes: and salute no man by the way.[149]

Q1LK38 And into whatsoever house ye enter, first say, Peace be to this house.[150]

Q1LK39 And if the son of peace be there, your peace shall rest upon it: if not, it shall turn to you again.[151]

Q1LK40 And in the same house remain, eating and drinking such things as they give: for the labourer is worthy of his hire. Go not from house to house.[152]

Q1LK41 And into whatsoever city ye enter, and they receive you, eat such things as are set before you:[153]

Q1LK42 And heal the sick that are therein, and say unto them, The kingdom of God is come nigh unto you.[154]

Q1LK43 But into whatsoever city ye enter, and they receive you not, go your ways out into the streets of the same, and say,[155]

Q1LK44 Even the very dust of your city, which cleaveth on us, we do wipe off against you: notwithstanding be ye sure of this, that the kingdom of God is come nigh unto you.[156]

Q1LK45 He that heareth you heareth me; and he that despiseth you despiseth me; and he that despiseth me despiseth him that sent me.[157]

Q1LK46 [Then Jesus said to His Disciples:] When ye pray, say, Our Father which art in heaven, Hallowed be thy name. Thy kingdom come. Thy will be done, as in heaven, so in earth.[158]

Q1LK47 Give us day by day our daily bread.[159]

Q1LK48 And forgive us our sins; for we also forgive every one that is indebted to us. And lead us not into temptation; but deliver us from evil.[160]

Q1LK49 And I say unto you, Ask, and it shall be given you; seek, and ye shall find; knock, and it shall be opened unto you.[161]

Q1LK50 For every one that asketh receiveth; and he that seeketh findeth; and to him that knocketh it shall be opened.[162]

Q1LK51 If a son shall ask bread of any of you that is a father, will he give him a stone? or if he ask a fish, will he for a fish give him a serpent?[163]

Q1LK52 Or if he shall ask an egg, will he offer him a scorpion?[164]

Q1LK53 If ye then, being evil, know how to give good gifts unto your children: how much more shall your heavenly Father give the Holy Spirit to them that ask him?[165]

Q1LK54 [Later, while Jesus was talking to His Disciples, He warned them about the hypocrisy of the Pharisees, saying:] For there is nothing covered, that shall not be revealed; neither hid, that shall not be known.[166]

Q1LK55 Therefore whatsoever ye have spoken in darkness shall be heard in the light; and that which ye have spoken in the ear in closets shall be proclaimed upon the housetops.[167]

Q1LK56 And I say unto you my friends, Be not afraid of them that kill the body, and after that have no more that they can do.[168]

Q1LK57 But I will forewarn you whom ye shall fear: Fear him, which after he hath killed hath power to cast into hell; yea, I say unto you, Fear him.[169]

Q1LK58 Are not five sparrows sold for two farthings, and not one of them is forgotten before God?[170]

Q1LK59 But even the very hairs of your head are all numbered. Fear not therefore: ye are of more value than many sparrows.[171]

Q1LK60 And when they bring you unto the synagogues, and unto magistrates, and powers, take ye no thought how or what thing ye shall answer, or what ye shall say:[172]

Q1LK61 For the Holy Ghost shall teach you in the same hour what ye ought to say.[173]

Q1LK62 [Jesus continued talking to His Disciples, saying:] Therefore I say unto you, Take no thought for your life, what ye shall eat; neither for the body, what ye shall put on.[174]

Q1LK63 The life is more than meat, and the body is more than raiment.[175]

Q1LK64 Consider the ravens: for they neither sow nor reap; which neither have storehouse nor barn; and God feedeth them: how much more are ye better than the fowls?[176]

Q1LK65 And which of you with taking thought can add to his stature one cubit?[177]

Q1LK66 If ye then be not able to do that thing which is least, why take ye thought for the rest?[178]

Q1LK67 Consider the lilies how they grow: they toil not, they spin not; and yet I say unto you, that Solomon in all his glory was not arrayed like one of these.[179]

Q1LK68 If then God so clothe the grass, which is to day in the field, and to morrow is cast into the oven; how much more will he clothe you, O ye of little faith?[180]

Q1LK69 And seek not ye what ye shall eat, or what ye shall drink, neither be ye of doubtful mind.[181]

Q1LK70 For all these things do the nations of the world seek after: and your Father knoweth that ye have need of these things.[182]

Q1LK71 But rather seek ye the kingdom of God; and all these things shall be added unto you.[183]

Q1LK72 Sell that ye have, and give alms; provide yourselves bags which wax not old, a treasure in the heavens that faileth not, where no thief approacheth, neither moth corrupteth.[184]

Q1LK73 For where your treasure is, there will your heart be

also.[185]

Q1LK74 Strive to enter in at the strait gate: for many, I say unto you, will seek to enter in, and shall not be able.[186]

Q1LK75 For whosoever exalteth himself shall be abased; and he that humbleth himself shall be exalted.[187]

Q1LK76 Then said he unto him, A certain man made a great supper, and bade many:[188]

Q1LK77 And sent his servant at supper time to say to them that were bidden, Come; for all things are now ready.[189]

Q1LK78 And they all with one consent began to make excuse. The first said unto him, I have bought a piece of ground, and I must needs go and see it: I pray thee have me excused.[190]

Q1LK79 And another said, I have bought five yoke of oxen, and I go to prove them: I pray thee have me excused.[191]

Q1LK80 And another said, I have married a wife, and therefore I cannot come.[192]

Q1LK81 So that servant came, and shewed his lord these things. Then the master of the house being angry said to his servant, Go out quickly into the streets and lanes of the city, and bring in hither the poor, and the maimed, and the halt, and the blind.[193]

Q1LK82 And the servant said, Lord, it is done as thou hast commanded, and yet there is room.[194]

Q1LK83 And the lord said unto the servant, Go out into the highways and hedges, and compel them to come in, that my house may be filled.[195]

Q1LK84 For I say unto you, That none of those men which were bidden shall taste of my supper.[196]

Q1LK85 If any man come to me, and hate not his father, and mother, and wife, and children, and brethren, and sisters, yea, and his own life also, he cannot be my disciple.[197]

Q1LK86 And whosoever doth not bear his cross, and come after me, cannot be my disciple.[198]

Q1LK87 Salt is good: but if the salt have lost his savour, wherewith shall it be seasoned? [199]

Q1LK88 It is neither fit for the land, nor yet for the dunghill; but men cast it out. He that hath ears to hear, let him hear.[200]

Q1LK89 Then said he unto the disciples, It is impossible but that offences will come: but woe unto him, through whom they come![201]

Q1LK90 It were better for him that a millstone were hanged about his neck, and he cast into the sea, than that he should offend one of these little ones.[202]

Q1LK91 If thy brother trespass against thee, rebuke him; and if he repent, forgive him.[203]

Q1LK92 And if he trespass against thee seven times in a day, and seven times in a day turn again to thee, saying, I repent; thou shalt forgive him.[204]

Q1LK93 And the apostles said unto the Lord, Increase our faith.[205]

Q1LK94 And the Lord said, If ye had faith as a grain of mustard seed, ye might say unto this sycamine tree, Be thou plucked up by the root, and be thou planted in the sea; and it should obey you.[206]

Q1LK95 Whosoever shall seek to save his life shall lose it; and whosoever shall lose his life shall preserve it.[207]

Q1LK96 I tell you, this man went down to his house justified rather than the other: for every one that exalteth himself shall be abased; and he that humbleth himself shall be exalted.[208]

2

Q² IN LUKE

THE SECOND LAYER OF THE GOSPEL OF Q
Q's Apocalyptic Teachings of Jesus in Luke

WRITTEN CIRCA A.D. 40s-50s
125 VERSES FROM THE KING JAMES VERSION[209]

KEY FOR SEABROOK NUMBERING SYSTEM
IN BRIEF: "Q2LK1": Gospel of Q, layer, canonical Gospel, verse.
IN DETAIL: "Q2LK1" means Gospel of Q, layer 2, as found in
   Gospel of Luke (KJV), first verse of layer 2.

Q2LK1 Then said he [John the Baptist] to the multitude that came forth to be baptized of him, O generation of vipers, who hath warned you to flee from the wrath to come?[210]

Q2LK2 Bring forth therefore fruits worthy of repentance, and begin not to say within yourselves, We have Abraham to our father: for I say unto you, That God is able of these stones to raise up children unto Abraham.[211]

Q2LK3 And now also the axe is laid unto the root of the trees: every tree therefore which bringeth not forth good fruit is hewn down, and cast into the fire.[212]

Q2LK4 John answered, saying unto them all, I indeed baptize you with water; but one mightier than I cometh, the latchet of whose shoes I am not worthy to unloose: he shall baptize you with the Holy Ghost and with fire:[213]

Q2LK5 Whose fan is in his hand, and he will throughly purge his floor, and will gather the wheat into his garner; but the chaff he will burn with fire unquenchable.[214]

Q2LK6 Now when he had ended all his sayings in the audience of the people, he entered into Capernaum.[215]

Q2LK7 And a certain centurion's servant, who was dear unto him, was sick, and ready to die.[216]

Q2LK8 And when he heard of Jesus, he sent unto him the elders of the Jews, beseeching him that he would come and heal his servant.[217]

Q2LK9 And when they came to Jesus, they besought him instantly, saying, That he was worthy for whom he should do this:[218]

Q2LK10 For he loveth our nation, and he hath built us a synagogue.[219]

Q2LK11 Then Jesus went with them. And when he was now not far from the house, the centurion sent friends to him, saying unto him, Lord, trouble not thyself: for I am not worthy that thou shouldest enter under my roof:[220]

Q2LK12 Wherefore neither thought I myself worthy to come unto thee: but say in a word, and my servant shall be healed.[221]

Q2LK13 For I also am a man set under authority, having under me soldiers, and I say unto one, Go, and he goeth; and to another, Come, and he cometh; and to my servant, Do this, and he doeth it.[222]

Q2LK14 When Jesus heard these things, he marvelled at him, and turned him about, and said unto the people that followed him, I say unto you, I have not found so great faith, no, not in Israel.[223]

Q2LK15 And they that were sent, returning to the house, found the servant whole that had been sick.[224]

Q2LK16 And the disciples of John [the Baptist] shewed him of all these things.[225]

Q2LK17 And John calling unto him two of his disciples sent them to Jesus, saying, Art thou he that should come? or look we for another?[226]

Q2LK18 When the men were come unto him, they said, John Baptist hath sent us unto thee, saying, Art thou he that should come? or look we for another?[227]

Q2LK19 And in that same hour he cured many of their infirmities and plagues, and of evil spirits; and unto many that were blind he gave sight.[228]

Q2LK20 Then Jesus answering said unto them, Go your way, and tell John what things ye have seen and heard; how that the blind see, the lame walk, the lepers are cleansed, the deaf hear, the dead are raised, to the poor the gospel is preached.[229]

Q2LK21 And blessed is he, whosoever shall not be offended in me.[230]

Q2LK22 And when the messengers of John were departed, he began to speak unto the people concerning John, What went ye out into the wilderness for to see? A reed shaken with the wind?[231]

Q2LK23 But what went ye out for to see? A man clothed in soft raiment? Behold, they which are gorgeously apparelled, and live delicately, are in kings' courts.[232]

Q2LK24 But what went ye out for to see? A prophet? Yea, I say unto you, and much more than a prophet.[233]

Q2LK25 This is he, of whom it is written, Behold, I send my messenger before thy face, which shall prepare thy way before thee.[234]

Q2LK26 For I say unto you, Among those that are born of women there is not a greater prophet than John the Baptist: but he that is least in the kingdom of God is greater than he.[235]

Q2LK27 And the Lord said, Whereunto then shall I liken the men of this generation? and to what are they like?[236]

Q2LK28 They are like unto children sitting in the marketplace, and calling one to another, and saying, We have piped unto you, and ye have not danced; we have mourned to you, and ye have not wept.[237]

Q2LK29 For John the Baptist came neither eating bread nor drinking wine; and ye say, He hath a devil.[238]

Q2LK30 The Son of man is come eating and drinking; and ye say, Behold a gluttonous man, and a winebibber, a friend of publicans and sinners![239]

Q2LK31 But wisdom is justified of all her children.[240]

Q2LK32 And he was casting out a devil, and it was dumb. And it came to pass, when the devil was gone out, the dumb spake; and the people wondered.[241]

Q2LK33 But some of them said, He casteth out devils through Beelzebub the chief of the devils.[242]

Q2LK34 And others, tempting him, sought of him a sign from heaven.[243]

Q2LK35 But he, knowing their thoughts, said unto them, Every kingdom divided against itself is brought to desolation; and a house divided against a house falleth.[244]

Q2LK36 If Satan also be divided against himself, how shall his kingdom stand? because ye say that I cast out devils through Beelzebub.[245]

Q2LK37 And if I by Beelzebub cast out devils, by whom do your sons cast them out? therefore shall they be your judges.[246]

Q2LK38 But if I with the finger of God cast out devils, no doubt the kingdom of God is come upon you.[247]

Q2LK39 When a strong man armed keepeth his palace, his goods are in peace:[248]

Q2LK40 But when a stronger than he shall come upon him, and overcome him, he taketh from him all his armour wherein he trusted, and divideth his spoils.[249]

Q2LK41 He that is not with me is against me: and he that gathereth not with me scattereth.[250]

Q2LK42 When the unclean spirit is gone out of a man, he walketh through dry places, seeking rest; and finding none, he saith, I will return unto my house whence I came out.[251]

Q2LK43 And when he cometh, he findeth it swept and garnished.[252]

Q2LK44 Then goeth he, and taketh to him seven other spirits more wicked than himself; and they enter in, and dwell there: and the last state of that man is worse than the first.[253]

Q2LK45 And it came to pass, as he spake these things, a certain woman of the company lifted up her voice, and said unto him, Blessed is the womb that bare thee, and the paps which thou hast sucked.[254]

Q2LK46 But he said, Yea rather, blessed are they that hear the word of God, and keep it.[255]

Q2LK47 And when the people were gathered thick together, he began to say, This is an evil generation: they seek a sign; and there shall no sign be given it, but the sign of Jonas the prophet.[256]

Q2LK48 For as Jonas was a sign unto the Ninevites, so shall also the Son of man be to this generation.[257]

Q2LK49 The queen of the south shall rise up in the judgment with the men of this generation, and condemn them: for she came from the utmost parts of the earth to hear the wisdom of Solomon; and, behold, a greater than Solomon is here.[258]

Q2LK50 The men of Nineve shall rise up in the judgment with this generation, and shall condemn it: for they repented at the preaching of Jonas; and, behold, a greater than Jonas is here.[259]

Q2LK51 No man, when he hath lighted a candle, putteth it in a secret place, neither under a bushel, but on a candlestick, that they which come in may see the light.[260]

Q2LK52 The light of the body is the eye: therefore when thine eye is single, thy whole body also is full of light; but when thine eye is evil, thy body also is full of darkness.[261]

Q2LK53 Take heed therefore that the light which is in thee be not darkness.[262]

Q2LK54 If thy whole body therefore be full of light, having no part dark, the whole shall be full of light, as when the bright shining of a candle doth give thee light.[263]

Q2LK55 [Jesus spoke to a Pharisee, saying,] Now do ye Pharisees make clean the outside of the cup and the platter; but your inward part is full of ravening and wickedness.[264]

Q2LK56 Ye fools, did not he that made that which is without make that which is within also?[265]

Q2LK57 But rather give alms of such things as ye have; and, behold, all things are clean unto you.[266]

Q2LK58 Ye tithe mint and rue and all manner of herbs, and pass over judgment and the love of God.[267]

Q2LK59 Woe unto you, Pharisees! for ye love the uppermost seats in the synagogues, and greetings in the markets.[268]

Q2LK60 Woe unto you, scribes and Pharisees, hypocrites! for ye are as graves which appear not, and the men that walk over them are not aware of them.[269]

Q2LK61 And he said, Woe unto you also, ye lawyers! for ye lade men with burdens grievous to be borne, and ye yourselves touch not the burdens with one of your fingers.[270]

Q2LK62 Woe unto you! for ye build the sepulchres of the prophets, and your fathers killed them.[271]

Q2LK63 Truly ye bear witness that ye allow the deeds of your fathers: for they indeed killed them, and ye build their sepulchres.[272]

Q2LK64 Therefore also said the wisdom of God, I will send them prophets and apostles, and some of them they shall slay and persecute:[273]

Q2LK65 That the blood of all the prophets, which was shed from the foundation of the world, may be required of this generation;[274]

Q2LK66 From the blood of Abel unto the blood of Zacharias, which perished between the altar and the temple: verily I say unto you, It shall be required of this generation.[275]

Q2LK67 Woe unto you, lawyers! for ye have taken away the key of knowledge: ye entered not in yourselves, and them that were entering in ye hindered.[276]

Q2LK68 And this know, that if the goodman of the house had

known what hour the thief would come, he would have watched, and not have suffered his house to be broken through.[277]

Q2LK69 Be ye therefore ready also: for the Son of man cometh at an hour when ye think not.[278]

Q2LK70 And the Lord said, Who then is that faithful and wise steward, whom his lord shall make ruler over his household, to give them their portion of meat in due season?[279]

Q2LK71 Blessed is that servant, whom his lord when he cometh shall find so doing.[280]

Q2LK72 Of a truth I say unto you, that he will make him ruler over all that he hath.[281]

Q2LK73 But and if that servant say in his heart, My lord delayeth his coming; and shall begin to beat the menservants and maidens, and to eat and drink, and to be drunken;[282]

Q2LK74 The lord of that servant will come in a day when he looketh not for him, and at an hour when he is not aware, and will cut him in sunder, and will appoint him his portion with the unbelievers.[283]

Q2LK75 I am come to send fire on the earth; and what will I, if it be already kindled?[284]

Q2LK76 Suppose ye that I am come to give peace on earth? I tell you, Nay; but rather division:[285]

Q2LK77 For from henceforth there shall be five in one house divided, three against two, and two against three.[286]

Q2LK78 The father shall be divided against the son, and the son against the father; the mother against the daughter, and the daughter against the mother; the mother in law against her daughter in law, and the daughter in law against her mother in law.[287]

Q2LK79 And he said also to the people, When ye see a cloud rise out of the west, straightway ye say, There cometh a shower; and so it is.[288]

Q2LK80 And when ye see the south wind blow, ye say, There will be heat; and it cometh to pass.[289]

Q2LK81 Ye hypocrites, ye can discern the face of the sky and of the earth; but how is it that ye do not discern this time?[290]

Q2LK82 Yea, and why even of yourselves judge ye not what is right?[291]

Q2LK83 When thou goest with thine adversary to the magistrate, as thou art in the way, give diligence that thou mayest be delivered from him; lest he hale thee to the judge, and the judge deliver thee to the officer, and the officer cast thee into prison.[292]

Q2LK84 I tell thee, thou shalt not depart thence, till thou hast paid the very last mite.[293]

Q2LK85 Then said he, Unto what is the kingdom of God like? and whereunto shall I resemble it?[294]

Q2LK86 It is like a grain of mustard seed, which a man took, and cast into his garden; and it grew, and waxed a great tree; and the fowls of the air lodged in the branches of it.[295]

Q2LK87 And again he said, Whereunto shall I liken the kingdom of God?[296]

Q2LK88 It is like leaven, which a woman took and hid in three measures of meal, till the whole was leavened.[297]

Q2LK89 Strive to enter in at the strait gate: for many, I say unto you, will seek to enter in, and shall not be able.[298]

Q2LK90 When once the master of the house is risen up, and hath shut to the door, and ye begin to stand without, and to knock at the door, saying, Lord, Lord, open unto us; and he shall answer and say unto you, I know you not whence ye are:[299]

Q2LK91 Then shall ye begin to say, We have eaten and drunk in thy presence, and thou hast taught in our streets.[300]

Q2LK92 But he shall say, I tell you, I know you not whence ye are; depart from me, all ye workers of iniquity.[301]

Q2LK93 There shall be weeping and gnashing of teeth, when ye shall see Abraham, and Isaac, and Jacob, and all the prophets, in the kingdom of God, and you yourselves thrust out.[302]

Q2LK94 And they shall come from the east, and from the west, and from the north, and from the south, and shall sit down in the kingdom of God.[303]

Q2LK95 And, behold, there are last which shall be first, and there are first which shall be last.[304]

Q2LK96 O Jerusalem, Jerusalem, which killest the prophets, and stonest them that are sent unto thee; how often would I have gathered thy children together, as a hen doth gather her brood under her wings, and ye would not![305]

Q2LK97 Behold, your house is left unto you desolate: and verily I say unto you, Ye shall not see me, until the time come when ye shall say, Blessed is he that cometh in the name of the Lord.[306]

Q2LK98 The law and the prophets were until John: since that time the kingdom of God is preached, and every man presseth into it.[307]

Q2LK99 And when he was demanded of the Pharisees, when the

kingdom of God should come, he answered them and said, The kingdom of God cometh not with observation:[308]

Q2LK100 Neither shall they say, Lo here! or, lo there! for, behold, the kingdom of God is within you.[309]

Q2LK101 [To His Disciples Jesus said:] And they shall say to you, See here; or, see there: go not after them, nor follow them.[310]

Q2LK102 For as the lightning, that lighteneth out of the one part under heaven, shineth unto the other part under heaven; so shall also the Son of man be in his day.[311]

Q2LK103 And as it was in the days of Noe [Noah], so shall it be also in the days of the Son of man.[312]

Q2LK104 They did eat, they drank, they married wives, they were given in marriage, until the day that Noe entered into the ark, and the flood came, and destroyed them all.[313]

Q2LK105 Likewise also as it was in the days of Lot; they did eat, they drank, they bought, they sold, they planted, they builded;[314]

Q2LK106 But the same day that Lot went out of Sodom it rained fire and brimstone from heaven, and destroyed them all.[315]

Q2LK107 Even thus shall it be in the day when the Son of man is revealed.[316]

Q2LK108 I tell you, in that night there shall be two men in one bed; the one shall be taken, and the other shall be left.[317]

Q2LK109 Two women shall be grinding together; the one shall be taken, and the other left.[318]

Q2LK110 He [Jesus] said therefore, A certain nobleman went into a far country to receive for himself a kingdom, and to return.[319]

Q2LK111 And he called his ten servants, and delivered them ten pounds, and said unto them, Occupy till I come.[320]

Q2LK112 But his citizens hated him, and sent a message after him, saying, We will not have this man to reign over us.[321]

Q2LK113 And it came to pass, that when he was returned, having received the kingdom, then he commanded these servants to be called unto him, to whom he had given the money, that he might know how much every man had gained by trading.[322]

Q2LK114 Then came the first, saying, Lord, thy pound hath gained ten pounds.[323]

Q2LK115 And he said unto him, Well, thou good servant: because thou hast been faithful in a very little, have thou authority over ten cities.[324]

Q2LK116 And the second came, saying, Lord, thy pound hath

gained five pounds.[325]

Q2LK117 And he said likewise to him, Be thou also over five cities.[326]

Q2LK118 And another came, saying, Lord, behold, here is thy pound, which I have kept laid up in a napkin:[327]

Q2LK119 For I feared thee, because thou art an austere man: thou takest up that thou layedst not down, and reapest that thou didst not sow.[328]

Q2LK120 And he saith unto him, Out of thine own mouth will I judge thee, thou wicked servant. Thou knewest that I was an austere man, taking up that I laid not down, and reaping that I did not sow:[329]

Q2LK121 Wherefore then gavest not thou my money into the bank, that at my coming I might have required mine own with usury?[330]

Q2LK122 And he said unto them that stood by, Take from him the pound, and give it to him that hath ten pounds.[331]

Q2LK123 (And they said unto him, Lord, he hath ten pounds.)[332]

Q2LK124 For I say unto you, That unto every one which hath shall be given; and from him that hath not, even that he hath shall be taken away from him.[333]

Q2LK125 But those mine enemies, which would not that I should reign over them, bring hither, and slay them before me.[334]

3

Q³ IN LUKE

THE THIRD LAYER OF THE GOSPEL OF Q
Q's Mythological Teachings of Jesus in Luke

WRITTEN CIRCA A.D. 75
21 VERSES FROM THE KING JAMES VERSION[335]

KEY FOR SEABROOK NUMBERING SYSTEM
IN BRIEF: "Q3LK1": Gospel of Q, layer, canonical Gospel, verse.
IN DETAIL: "Q3LK1" means Gospel of Q, layer 3, as found in
Gospel of Luke (KJV), first verse of layer 3.

Q3LK1 And Jesus being full of the Holy Ghost returned from Jordan, and was led by the Spirit into the wilderness,[336]

Q3LK2 Being forty days tempted of the devil. And in those days he did eat nothing: and when they were ended, he afterward hungered.[337]

Q3LK3 And the devil said unto him, If thou be the Son of God, command this stone that it be made bread.[338]

Q3LK4 And Jesus answered him, saying, It is written, That man shall not live by bread alone, but by every word of God.[339]

Q3LK5 And the devil, taking him up into an high mountain, shewed unto him all the kingdoms of the world in a moment of time.[340]

Q3LK6 And the devil said unto him, All this power will I give thee, and the glory of them: for that is delivered unto me; and to whomsoever I will I give it.[341]

Q3LK7 If thou therefore wilt worship me, all shall be thine.[342]

Q3LK8 And Jesus answered and said unto him, Get thee behind me, Satan: for it is written, Thou shalt worship the Lord thy God, and him only shalt thou serve. [343]

Q3LK9 And he [the Devil] brought him to Jerusalem, and set him on a pinnacle of the temple, and said unto him, If thou be the Son of God, cast thyself down from hence: [344]

Q3LK10 For it is written, He shall give his angels charge over thee, to keep thee: [345]

Q3LK11 And in their hands they shall bear thee up, lest at any time thou dash thy foot against a stone. [346]

Q3LK12 And Jesus answering said unto him, It is said, Thou shalt not tempt the Lord thy God. [347]

Q3LK13 And when the devil had ended all the temptation, he departed from him for a season. [348]

Q3LK14 In that hour Jesus rejoiced in spirit, and said, I thank thee, O Father, Lord of heaven and earth, that thou hast hid these things from the wise and prudent, and hast revealed them unto babes: even so, Father; for so it seemed good in thy sight. [349]

Q3LK15 All things are delivered to me of my Father: and no man knoweth who the Son is, but the Father; and who the Father is, but the Son, and he to whom the Son will reveal him. [350]

Q3LK16 . . . these ought ye to have done, and not to leave the other undone. [351]

Q3LK17 And it is easier for heaven and earth to pass, than one tittle of the law to fail. [352]

Q3LK18 Whosoever putteth away his wife, and marrieth another, committeth adultery: and whosoever marrieth her that is put away from her husband committeth adultery. [353]

Q3LK19 Ye are they which have continued with me in my temptations. [354]

Q3LK20 And I appoint unto you a kingdom, as my Father hath appointed unto me; [355]

Q3LK21 That ye may eat and drink at my table in my kingdom, and sit on thrones judging the twelve tribes of Israel. [356]

4

Q⁶ IN LUKE

Q¹, Q², AND Q³ COMBINED
The Complete Gospel of Q in Luke

WRITTEN CIRCA A.D. 30s-75
240 VERSES FROM THE KING JAMES VERSION[357]

KEY FOR SEABROOK NUMBERING SYSTEM
IN BRIEF: "QCLK1": Gospel of Q, canonical Gospel, verse.
IN DETAIL: "QCLK1" means Gospel of Q, complete, as found in
Gospel of Luke (KJV), first verse of complete edition.

QCLK1 This is part of the true and original Gospel of the Kingdom as taught by Jesus.[358]

QCLK2 Then said he [John the Baptist] to the multitude that came forth to be baptized of him, O generation of vipers, who hath warned you to flee from the wrath to come?[359]

QCLK3 Bring forth therefore fruits worthy of repentance, and begin not to say within yourselves, We have Abraham to our father: for I say unto you, That God is able of these stones to raise up children unto Abraham.[360]

QCLK4 And now also the axe is laid unto the root of the trees: every tree therefore which bringeth not forth good fruit is hewn down, and cast into the fire.[361]

QCLK5 John answered, saying unto them all, I indeed baptize you with water; but one mightier than I cometh, the latchet of whose shoes I am not worthy to unloose: he shall baptize you with the Holy Ghost and with fire:[362]

QCLK6 Whose fan is in his hand, and he will throughly purge his floor, and will gather the wheat into his garner; but the chaff he will burn with fire unquenchable.[363]

QCLK7 And Jesus being full of the Holy Ghost returned from Jordan, and was led by the Spirit into the wilderness,[364]

QCLK8 Being forty days tempted of the devil. And in those days he did eat nothing: and when they were ended, he afterward hungered.[365]

QCLK9 And the devil said unto him, If thou be the Son of God, command this stone that it be made bread.[366]

QCLK10 And Jesus answered him, saying, It is written, That man shall not live by bread alone, but by every word of God.[367]

QCLK11 And the devil, taking him up into an high mountain, shewed unto him all the kingdoms of the world in a moment of time.[368]

QCLK12 And the devil said unto him, All this power will I give thee, and the glory of them: for that is delivered unto me; and to whomsoever I will I give it.[369]

QCLK13 If thou therefore wilt worship me, all shall be thine.[370]

QCLK14 And Jesus answered and said unto him, Get thee behind me, Satan: for it is written, Thou shalt worship the Lord thy God, and him only shalt thou serve.[371]

QCLK15 And he brought him to Jerusalem, and set him on a pinnacle of the temple, and said unto him, If thou be the Son of God, cast thyself down from hence:[372]

QCLK16 For it is written, He shall give his angels charge over thee, to keep thee:[373]

QCLK17 And in their hands they shall bear thee up, lest at any time thou dash thy foot against a stone.[374]

QCLK18 And Jesus answering said unto him, It is said, Thou shalt not tempt the Lord thy God.[375]

QCLK19 And when the devil had ended all the temptation, he departed from him for a season.[376]

QCLK20 [Speaking to His Disciples, Jesus said:] Blessed be ye poor: for yours is the kingdom of God.[377]

QCLK21 Blessed are ye that hunger now: for ye shall be filled. Blessed are ye that weep now: for ye shall laugh.[378]

QCLK22 Blessed are ye, when men shall hate you, and when they shall separate you from their company, and shall reproach you, and cast out your name as evil, for the Son of man's sake.[379]

QCLK23 For, behold, your reward is great in heaven.[380]

QCLK24 But I say unto you which hear, Love your enemies, do good to them which hate you,[381]

QCLK25 Bless them that curse you, and pray for them which despitefully use you.[382]

QCLK26 And unto him that smiteth thee on the one cheek offer also the other; and him that taketh away thy cloke forbid not to take thy coat also.[383]

QCLK27 Give to every man that asketh of thee; and of him that taketh away thy goods ask them not again.[384]

QCLK28 And as ye would that men should do to you, do ye also to them likewise.[385]

QCLK29 For if ye love them which love you, what thank have ye? for sinners also love those that love them.[386]

QCLK30 And if ye do good to them which do good to you, what thank have ye? for sinners also do even the same.[387]

QCLK31 And if ye lend to them of whom ye hope to receive, what thank have ye? for sinners also lend to sinners, to receive as much again.[388]

QCLK32 But love ye your enemies, and do good, and lend, hoping for nothing again; and your reward shall be great, and ye shall be the children of the Highest: for he is kind unto the unthankful and to the evil.[389]

QCLK33 Be ye therefore merciful, as your Father also is merciful.[390]

QCLK34 Judge not, and ye shall not be judged: condemn not, and ye shall not be condemned: forgive, and ye shall be forgiven:[391]

QCLK35 Give, and it shall be given unto you; good measure, pressed down, and shaken together, and running over, shall men give into your bosom. For with the same measure that ye mete withal it shall be measured to you again.[392]

QCLK36 And he spake a parable unto them, Can the blind lead the blind? shall they not both fall into the ditch?[393]

QCLK37 The disciple is not above his master: but every one that is perfect shall be as his master.[394]

QCLK38 And why beholdest thou the mote that is in thy brother's eye, but perceivest not the beam that is in thine own eye?[395]

QCLK39 Either how canst thou say to thy brother, Brother, let me pull out the mote that is in thine eye, when thou thyself beholdest not the beam that is in thine own eye? Thou hypocrite, cast out first the beam out of thine own eye, and then shalt thou see clearly to pull out the mote that is in thy brother's eye.[396]

QCLK40 For a good tree bringeth not forth corrupt fruit; neither doth a corrupt tree bring forth good fruit.[397]

QCLK41 For every tree is known by his own fruit. For of thorns men do not gather figs, nor of a bramble bush gather they grapes.[398]

QCLK42 A good man out of the good treasure of his heart bringeth forth that which is good; and an evil man out of the evil treasure of his heart bringeth forth that which is evil: for of the abundance of the heart his mouth speaketh.[399]

QCLK43 And why call ye me, Lord, Lord, and do not the things which I say?[400]

QCLK44 Whosoever cometh to me, and heareth my sayings, and doeth them, I will shew you to whom he is like:[401]

QCLK45 He is like a man which built an house, and digged deep, and laid the foundation on a rock: and when the flood arose, the stream beat vehemently upon that house, and could not shake it: for it was founded upon a rock.[402]

QCLK46 But he that heareth, and doeth not, is like a man that without a foundation built an house upon the earth; against which the stream did beat vehemently, and immediately it fell; and the ruin of that house was great.[403]

QCLK47 Now when he had ended all his sayings in the audience of the people, he entered into Capernaum.[404]

QCLK48 And a certain centurion's servant, who was dear unto him, was sick, and ready to die.[405]

QCLK49 And when he heard of Jesus, he sent unto him the elders of the Jews, beseeching him that he would come and heal his servant.[406]

QCLK50 And when they came to Jesus, they besought him instantly, saying, That he was worthy for whom he should do this:[407]

QCLK51 For he loveth our nation, and he hath built us a synagogue.[408]

QCLK52 Then Jesus went with them. And when he was now not far from the house, the centurion sent friends to him, saying unto him, Lord, trouble not thyself: for I am not worthy that thou shouldest enter under my roof:[409]

QCLK53 Wherefore neither thought I myself worthy to come unto thee: but say in a word, and my servant shall be healed.[410]

QCLK54 For I also am a man set under authority, having under me soldiers, and I say unto one, Go, and he goeth; and to another, Come, and he cometh; and to my servant, Do this, and he doeth it.[411]

QCLK55 When Jesus heard these things, he marvelled at him, and turned him about, and said unto the people that followed him, I say unto you, I have not found so great faith, no, not in Israel.[412]

QCLK56 And they that were sent, returning to the house, found the servant whole that had been sick.[413]

QCLK57 And the disciples of John shewed him of all these things.[414]

QCLK58 And John calling unto him two of his disciples sent them to Jesus, saying, Art thou he that should come? or look we for another?[415]

QCLK59 When the men were come unto him, they said, John Baptist hath sent us unto thee, saying, Art thou he that should come? or look we for another?[416]

QCLK60 And in that same hour he cured many of their infirmities and plagues, and of evil spirits; and unto many that were blind he gave sight.[417]

QCLK61 Then Jesus answering said unto them, Go your way, and tell John what things ye have seen and heard; how that the blind see, the lame walk, the lepers are cleansed, the deaf hear, the dead are raised, to the poor the gospel is preached.[418]

QCLK62 And blessed is he, whosoever shall not be offended in me.[419]

QCLK63 And when the messengers of John were departed, he began to speak unto the people concerning John, What went ye out into the wilderness for to see? A reed shaken with the wind?[420]

QCLK64 But what went ye out for to see? A man clothed in soft raiment? Behold, they which are gorgeously apparelled, and live delicately, are in kings' courts.[421]

QCLK65 But what went ye out for to see? A prophet? Yea, I say unto you, and much more than a prophet.[422]

QCLK66 This is he, of whom it is written, Behold, I send my messenger before thy face, which shall prepare thy way before thee.[423]

QCLK67 For I say unto you, Among those that are born of women there is not a greater prophet than John the Baptist: but he that is least in the kingdom of God is greater than he.[424]

QCLK68 And the Lord said, Whereunto then shall I liken the men of this generation? and to what are they like?[425]

QCLK69 They are like unto children sitting in the marketplace, and calling one to another, and saying, We have piped unto you, and ye have not danced; we have mourned to you, and ye have not wept.[426]

QCLK70 For John the Baptist came neither eating bread nor drinking wine; and ye say, He hath a devil.[427]

QCLK71 The Son of man is come eating and drinking; and ye say, Behold a gluttonous man, and a winebibber, a friend of publicans and sinners![428]

QCLK72 But wisdom is justified of all her children.[429]

QCLK73 And it came to pass, that, as they went in the way, a certain man said unto him, Lord, I will follow thee whithersoever thou goest.[430]

QCLK74 And Jesus said unto him, Foxes have holes, and birds of the air have nests; but the Son of man hath not where to lay his head.[431]

QCLK75 And he said unto another, Follow me. But he said, Lord, suffer me first to go and bury my father.[432]

QCLK76 Jesus said unto him, Let the dead bury their dead: but go thou and preach the kingdom of God.[433]

QCLK77 And another also said, Lord, I will follow thee; but let me first go bid them farewell, which are at home at my house.[434]

QCLK78 And Jesus said unto him, No man, having put his hand to the plough, and looking back, is fit for the kingdom of God.[435]

QCLK79 [Speaking to His disciples, Jesus said:] The harvest truly is great, but the labourers are few: pray ye therefore the Lord of the harvest, that he would send forth labourers into his harvest.[436]

QCLK80 Go your ways: behold, I send you forth as lambs among wolves.[437]

QCLK81 Carry neither purse, nor scrip, nor shoes: and salute no man by the way.[438]

QCLK82 And into whatsoever house ye enter, first say, Peace be to this house.[439]

QCLK83 And if the son of peace be there, your peace shall rest upon it: if not, it shall turn to you again.[440]

QCLK84 And in the same house remain, eating and drinking such things as they give: for the labourer is worthy of his hire. Go not from house to house.[441]

QCLK85 And into whatsoever city ye enter, and they receive you, eat such things as are set before you:[442]

QCLK86 And heal the sick that are therein, and say unto them, The kingdom of God is come nigh unto you.[443]

QCLK87 But into whatsoever city ye enter, and they receive you not, go your ways out into the streets of the same, and say,[444]

QCLK88 Even the very dust of your city, which cleaveth on us, we do wipe off against you: notwithstanding be ye sure of this, that the kingdom of God is come nigh unto you.[445]

QCLK89 He that heareth you heareth me; and he that despiseth you despiseth me; and he that despiseth me despiseth him that sent me.[446]

QCLK90 In that hour Jesus rejoiced in spirit, and said, I thank thee, O Father, Lord of heaven and earth, that thou hast hid these things from the wise and prudent, and hast revealed them unto babes: even so, Father; for so it seemed good in thy sight.[447]

QCLK91 All things are delivered to me of my Father: and no man knoweth who the Son is, but the Father; and who the Father is, but the Son, and he to whom the Son will reveal him.[448]

QCLK92 Then Jesus said to His Disciples: When ye pray, say, Our Father which art in heaven, Hallowed be thy name. Thy kingdom come. Thy will be done, as in heaven, so in earth.[449]

QCLK93 Give us day by day our daily bread.[450]

QCLK94 And forgive us our sins; for we also forgive every one that is indebted to us. And lead us not into temptation; but deliver us from evil.[451]

QCLK95 And I say unto you, Ask, and it shall be given you; seek, and ye shall find; knock, and it shall be opened unto you.[452]

QCLK96 For every one that asketh receiveth; and he that seeketh findeth; and to him that knocketh it shall be opened.[453]

QCLK97 If a son shall ask bread of any of you that is a father, will he give him a stone? or if he ask a fish, will he for a fish give him a serpent?[454]

QCLK98 Or if he shall ask an egg, will he offer him a scorpion?[455]

QCLK99 If ye then, being evil, know how to give good gifts unto your children: how much more shall your heavenly Father give the Holy Spirit to them that ask him?[456]

QCLK100 And he was casting out a devil, and it was dumb. And it came to pass, when the devil was gone out, the dumb spake; and the people wondered.[457]

QCLK101 But some of them said, He casteth out devils through Beelzebub the chief of the devils.[458]

QCLK102 And others, tempting him, sought of him a sign from heaven.[459]

QCLK103 But he, knowing their thoughts, said unto them, Every kingdom divided against itself is brought to desolation; and a house divided against a house falleth.[460]

QCLK104 If Satan also be divided against himself, how shall his kingdom stand? because ye say that I cast out devils through Beelzebub.[461]

QCLK105 And if I by Beelzebub cast out devils, by whom do your sons cast them out? therefore shall they be your judges.[462]

QCLK106 But if I with the finger of God cast out devils, no doubt the kingdom of God is come upon you.[463]

QCLK107 When a strong man armed keepeth his palace, his goods are in peace:[464]

QCLK108 But when a stronger than he shall come upon him, and overcome him, he taketh from him all his armour wherein he trusted, and divideth his spoils.[465]

QCLK109 He that is not with me is against me: and he that gathereth not with me scattereth.[466]

QCLK110 When the unclean spirit is gone out of a man, he walketh through dry places, seeking rest; and finding none, he saith, I will return unto my house whence I came out.[467]

QCLK111 And when he cometh, he findeth it swept and garnished.[468]

QCLK112 Then goeth he, and taketh to him seven other spirits more wicked than himself; and they enter in, and dwell there: and the last state of that man is worse than the first.[469]

QCLK113 And it came to pass, as he spake these things, a certain woman of the company lifted up her voice, and said unto him, Blessed is the womb that bare thee, and the paps which thou hast sucked.[470]

QCLK114 But he said, Yea rather, blessed are they that hear the word of God, and keep it.[471]

QCLK115 And when the people were gathered thick together, he began to say, This is an evil generation: they seek a sign; and there shall no sign be given it, but the sign of Jonas the prophet.[472]

QCLK116 For as Jonas was a sign unto the Ninevites, so shall also the Son of man be to this generation.[473]

QCLK117 The queen of the south shall rise up in the judgment with the men of this generation, and condemn them: for she came from the utmost parts of the earth to hear the wisdom of Solomon; and, behold, a greater than Solomon is here.[474]

QCLK118 The men of Nineve shall rise up in the judgment with this generation, and shall condemn it: for they repented at the preaching of Jonas; and, behold, a greater than Jonas is here.[475]

QCLK119 No man, when he hath lighted a candle, putteth it in a secret place, neither under a bushel, but on a candlestick, that they which come in may see the light.[476]

QCLK120 The light of the body is the eye: therefore when thine eye is single, thy whole body also is full of light; but when thine eye is evil, thy body also is full of darkness.[477]

QCLK121 Take heed therefore that the light which is in thee be not darkness.[478]

QCLK122 If thy whole body therefore be full of light, having no part dark, the whole shall be full of light, as when the bright shining of a candle doth give thee light.[479]

QCLK123 [Jesus spoke to a Pharisee, saying,] Now do ye Pharisees make clean the outside of the cup and the platter; but your inward part is full of ravening and wickedness.[480]

QCLK124 Ye fools, did not he that made that which is without make that which is within also?[481]

QCLK125 But rather give alms of such things as ye have; and, behold, all things are clean unto you.[482]

QCLK126 For ye tithe mint and rue and all manner of herbs, and pass over judgment and the love of God: these ought ye to have done, and not to leave the other undone.[483]

QCLK127 Woe unto you, Pharisees! for ye love the uppermost seats in the synagogues, and greetings in the markets.[484]

QCLK128 Woe unto you, scribes and Pharisees, hypocrites! for ye are as graves which appear not, and the men that walk over them are not aware of them.[485]

QCLK129 And he said, Woe unto you also, ye lawyers! for ye lade men with burdens grievous to be borne, and ye yourselves touch not the burdens with one of your fingers.[486]

QCLK130 Woe unto you! for ye build the sepulchres of the prophets, and your fathers killed them.[487]

QCLK131 Truly ye bear witness that ye allow the deeds of your fathers: for they indeed killed them, and ye build their sepulchres.[488]

QCLK132 Therefore also said the wisdom of God, I will send them prophets and apostles, and some of them they shall slay and persecute:[489]

QCLK133 That the blood of all the prophets, which was shed from the foundation of the world, may be required of this generation;[490]

QCLK134 From the blood of Abel unto the blood of Zacharias, which perished between the altar and the temple: verily I say unto you, It shall be required of this generation.[491]

QCLK135 Woe unto you, lawyers! for ye have taken away the key of knowledge: ye entered not in yourselves, and them that were entering in ye hindered.[492]

QCLK136 [Later, while Jesus was talking to His Disciples, He warned them about the hypocrisy of the Pharisees, saying:] For there is nothing covered, that shall not be revealed; neither hid, that shall not be known.[493]

QCLK137 Therefore whatsoever ye have spoken in darkness shall be heard in the light; and that which ye have spoken in the ear in closets shall be proclaimed upon the housetops.[494]

QCLK138 And I say unto you my friends, Be not afraid of them that kill the body, and after that have no more that they can do.[495]

QCLK139 But I will forewarn you whom ye shall fear: Fear him, which after he hath killed hath power to cast into hell; yea, I say unto you, Fear him.[496]

QCLK140 Are not five sparrows sold for two farthings, and not one of them is forgotten before God?[497]

QCLK141 But even the very hairs of your head are all numbered. Fear not therefore: ye are of more value than many sparrows.[498]

QCLK142 And when they bring you unto the synagogues, and unto magistrates, and powers, take ye no thought how or what thing ye shall answer, or what ye shall say:[499]

QCLK143 For the Holy Ghost shall teach you in the same hour what ye ought to say.[500]

QCLK144 [Jesus continued talking to His Disciples, saying:] Therefore I say unto you, Take no thought for your life, what ye shall eat; neither for the body, what ye shall put on.[501]

QCLK145 The life is more than meat, and the body is more than raiment.[502]

QCLK146 Consider the ravens: for they neither sow nor reap; which neither have storehouse nor barn; and God feedeth them: how much more are ye better than the fowls?[503]

QCLK147 And which of you with taking thought can add to his stature one cubit?[504]

QCLK148 If ye then be not able to do that thing which is least, why take ye thought for the rest?[505]

QCLK149 Consider the lilies how they grow: they toil not, they spin not; and yet I say unto you, that Solomon in all his glory was not arrayed like one of these.[506]

QCLK150 If then God so clothe the grass, which is to day in the field, and to morrow is cast into the oven; how much more will he clothe you, O ye of little faith?[507]

QCLK151 And seek not ye what ye shall eat, or what ye shall drink, neither be ye of doubtful mind.[508]

QCLK152 For all these things do the nations of the world seek after: and your Father knoweth that ye have need of these things.[509]

QCLK153 But rather seek ye the kingdom of God; and all these things shall be added unto you.[510]

QCLK154 Sell that ye have, and give alms; provide yourselves bags which wax not old, a treasure in the heavens that faileth not, where no thief approacheth, neither moth corrupteth.[511]

QCLK155 For where your treasure is, there will your heart be also.[512]

QCLK156 And this know, that if the goodman of the house had known what hour the thief would come, he would have watched, and not have suffered his house to be broken through.[513]

QCLK157 Be ye therefore ready also: for the Son of man cometh at an hour when ye think not.[514]

QCLK158 And the Lord said, Who then is that faithful and wise steward, whom his lord shall make ruler over his household, to give them their portion of meat in due season?[515]

QCLK159 Blessed is that servant, whom his lord when he cometh shall find so doing.[516]

QCLK160 Of a truth I say unto you, that he will make him ruler over all that he hath.[517]

QCLK161 But and if that servant say in his heart, My lord delayeth his coming; and shall begin to beat the menservants and maidens, and to eat and drink, and to be drunken;[518]

QCLK162 The lord of that servant will come in a day when he looketh not for him, and at an hour when he is not aware, and will cut him in sunder, and will appoint him his portion with the unbelievers.[519]

QCLK163 I am come to send fire on the earth; and what will I, if it be already kindled?[520]

QCLK164 Suppose ye that I am come to give peace on earth? I tell you, Nay; but rather division:[521]

QCLK165 For from henceforth there shall be five in one house divided, three against two, and two against three.[522]

QCLK166 The father shall be divided against the son, and the son against the father; the mother against the daughter, and the daughter against the mother; the mother in law against her daughter in law, and the daughter in law against her mother in law.[523]

QCLK167 And he said also to the people, When ye see a cloud rise out of the west, straightway ye say, There cometh a shower; and so it is.[524]

QCLK168 And when ye see the south wind blow, ye say, There will be heat; and it cometh to pass.[525]

QCLK169 Ye hypocrites, ye can discern the face of the sky and of the earth; but how is it that ye do not discern this time?[526]

QCLK170 Yea, and why even of yourselves judge ye not what is right?[527]

QCLK171 When thou goest with thine adversary to the magistrate, as thou art in the way, give diligence that thou mayest be delivered from him; lest he hale thee to the judge, and the judge deliver thee to the officer, and the officer cast thee into prison.[528]

QCLK172 I tell thee, thou shalt not depart thence, till thou hast paid the very last mite.[529]

QCLK173 Then said he, Unto what is the kingdom of God like? and whereunto shall I resemble it?[530]

QCLK174 It is like a grain of mustard seed, which a man took, and cast into his garden; and it grew, and waxed a great tree; and the fowls of the air lodged in the branches of it.[531]

QCLK175 And again he said, Whereunto shall I liken the kingdom of God?[532]

QCLK176 It is like leaven, which a woman took and hid in three measures of meal, till the whole was leavened.[533]

QCLK177 Strive to enter in at the strait gate: for many, I say unto you, will seek to enter in, and shall not be able.[534]

QCLK178 When once the master of the house is risen up, and hath shut to the door, and ye begin to stand without, and to knock at the door, saying, Lord, Lord, open unto us; and he shall answer and say unto you, I know you not whence ye are:[535]

QCLK179 Then shall ye begin to say, We have eaten and drunk in thy presence, and thou hast taught in our streets.[536]

QCLK180 But he shall say, I tell you, I know you not whence ye are; depart from me, all ye workers of iniquity.[537]

QCLK181 There shall be weeping and gnashing of teeth, when ye shall see Abraham, and Isaac, and Jacob, and all the prophets, in the kingdom of God, and you yourselves thrust out.[538]

QCLK182 And they shall come from the east, and from the west, and from the north, and from the south, and shall sit down in the kingdom of God.[539]

QCLK183 And, behold, there are last which shall be first, and there are first which shall be last.[540]

QCLK184 O Jerusalem, Jerusalem, which killest the prophets, and stonest them that are sent unto thee; how often would I have gathered thy children together, as a hen doth gather her brood under her wings, and ye would not![541]

QCLK185 Behold, your house is left unto you desolate: and verily I say unto you, Ye shall not see me, until the time come when ye shall say, Blessed is he that cometh in the name of the Lord.[542]

QCLK186 For whosoever exalteth himself shall be abased; and he that humbleth himself shall be exalted.[543]

QCLK187 Then said he unto him, A certain man made a great supper, and bade many:[544]

QCLK188 And sent his servant at supper time to say to them that were bidden, Come; for all things are now ready.[545]

QCLK189 And they all with one consent began to make excuse. The first said unto him, I have bought a piece of ground, and I must needs go and see it: I pray thee have me excused.[546]

QCLK190 And another said, I have bought five yoke of oxen, and I go to prove them: I pray thee have me excused.[547]

QCLK191 And another said, I have married a wife, and therefore I cannot come.[548]

QCLK192 So that servant came, and shewed his lord these things. Then the master of the house being angry said to his servant, Go out quickly into the streets and lanes of the city, and bring in hither the poor, and the maimed, and the halt, and the blind.[549]

QCLK193 And the servant said, Lord, it is done as thou hast commanded, and yet there is room.[550]

QCLK194 And the lord said unto the servant, Go out into the highways and hedges, and compel them to come in, that my house may be filled.[551]

QCLK195 For I say unto you, That none of those men which were bidden shall taste of my supper.[552]

QCLK196 If any man come to me, and hate not his father, and mother, and wife, and children, and brethren, and sisters, yea, and his own life also, he cannot be my disciple.[553]

QCLK197 And whosoever doth not bear his cross, and come after me, cannot be my disciple.[554]

QCLK198 Salt is good: but if the salt have lost his savour, wherewith shall it be seasoned?[555]

QCLK199 It is neither fit for the land, nor yet for the dunghill; but men cast it out. He that hath ears to hear, let him hear.[556]

QCLK200 The law and the prophets were until John: since that time the kingdom of God is preached, and every man presseth into it.[557]

QCLK201 And it is easier for heaven and earth to pass, than one tittle of the law to fail.[558]

QCLK202 Whosoever putteth away his wife, and marrieth another, committeth adultery: and whosoever marrieth her that is put away from her husband committeth adultery.[559]

QCLK203 Then said he unto the disciples, It is impossible but that offences will come: but woe unto him, through whom they come![560]

QCLK204 It were better for him that a millstone were hanged about his neck, and he cast into the sea, than that he should offend one of these little ones.[561]

QCLK205 If thy brother trespass against thee, rebuke him; and if he repent, forgive him.[562]

QCLK206 And if he trespass against thee seven times in a day, and seven times in a day turn again to thee, saying, I repent; thou shalt forgive him.[563]

QCLK207 And the apostles said unto the Lord, Increase our faith.[564]

QCLK208 And the Lord said, If ye had faith as a grain of mustard seed, ye might say unto this sycamine tree, Be thou plucked up by the root, and be thou planted in the sea; and it should obey you.[565]

QCLK209 And when he was demanded of the Pharisees, when the kingdom of God should come, he answered them and said, The kingdom of God cometh not with observation:[566]

QCLK210 Neither shall they say, Lo here! or, lo there! for, behold, the kingdom of God is within you.[567]

QCLK211 [To His Disciples Jesus said:] And they shall say to you, See here; or, see there: go not after them, nor follow them.[568]

QCLK212 For as the lightning, that lighteneth out of the one part under heaven, shineth unto the other part under heaven; so shall also the Son of man be in his day.[569]

QCLK213 And as it was in the days of Noe [Noah], so shall it be also in the days of the Son of man.[570]

QCLK214 They did eat, they drank, they married wives, they were given in marriage, until the day that Noe entered into the ark, and the flood came, and destroyed them all.[571]

QCLK215 Likewise also as it was in the days of Lot; they did eat, they drank, they bought, they sold, they planted, they builded;[572]

QCLK216 But the same day that Lot went out of Sodom it rained fire and brimstone from heaven, and destroyed them all.[573]

QCLK217 Even thus shall it be in the day when the Son of man is revealed.[574]

QCLK218 Whosoever shall seek to save his life shall lose it; and whosoever shall lose his life shall preserve it.[575]

QCLK219 I tell you, in that night there shall be two men in one bed; the one shall be taken, and the other shall be left.[576]

QCLK220 Two women shall be grinding together; the one shall be taken, and the other left.[577]

QCLK221 I tell you, this man went down to his house justified rather than the other: for every one that exalteth himself shall be abased; and he that humbleth himself shall be exalted.[578]

QCLK222 He said [to the crowd] therefore, A certain nobleman went into a far country to receive for himself a kingdom, and to return.[579]

QCLK223 And he called his ten servants, and delivered them ten pounds, and said unto them, Occupy till I come.[580]

QCLK224 But his citizens hated him, and sent a message after him, saying, We will not have this man to reign over us.[581]

QCLK225 And it came to pass, that when he was returned, having received the kingdom, then he commanded these servants to be called unto him, to whom he had given the money, that he might know how much every man had gained by trading.[582]

QCLK226 Then came the first, saying, Lord, thy pound hath gained ten pounds.[583]

QCLK227 And he said unto him, Well, thou good servant: because thou hast been faithful in a very little, have thou authority over ten cities.[584]

QCLK228 And the second came, saying, Lord, thy pound hath gained five pounds.[585]

QCLK229 And he said likewise to him, Be thou also over five cities.[586]

QCLK230 And another came, saying, Lord, behold, here is thy pound, which I have kept laid up in a napkin:[587]

QCLK231 For I feared thee, because thou art an austere man: thou takest up that thou layedst not down, and reapest that thou didst not sow.[588]

QCLK232 And he saith unto him, Out of thine own mouth will I judge thee, thou wicked servant. Thou knewest that I was an austere man, taking up that I laid not down, and reaping that I did not sow:[589]

QCLK233 Wherefore then gavest not thou my money into the bank, that at my coming I might have required mine own with usury?[590]

QCLK234 And he said unto them that stood by, Take from him the pound, and give it to him that hath ten pounds.[591]

QCLK235 (And they said unto him, Lord, he hath ten pounds.)[592]

QCLK236 For I say unto you, That unto every one which hath shall be given; and from him that hath not, even that he hath shall be taken away from him.[593]

QCLK237 But those mine enemies, which would not that I should reign over them, bring hither, and slay them before me.[594]

QCLK238 Ye are they which have continued with me in my temptations.[595]

QCLK239 And I appoint unto you a kingdom, as my Father hath appointed unto me;[596]

QCLK240 That ye may eat and drink at my table in my kingdom, and sit on thrones judging the twelve tribes of Israel.[597]

SECTION 2

THE GOSPEL OF Q
ACCORDING TO MARK & MATTHEW

5

Q⁶ IN MARK

THE COMPLETE GOSPEL OF Q IN MARK

WRITTEN CIRCA A.D. 30s-70s
36 VERSES FROM THE KING JAMES VERSION[598]

KEY FOR SEABROOK NUMBERING SYSTEM
IN BRIEF: "QCMK1": Gospel of Q, canonical Gospel, verse.
IN DETAIL: "QCMK1" means Gospel of Q, complete, as found in
Gospel of Mark (KJV), first verse of complete edition.

QCMK1   This is part of the true and original Gospel of the Kingdom as taught by Jesus.[599]

QCMK2   As it is written in the prophets, Behold, I send my messenger before thy face, which shall prepare thy way before thee.[600]

QCMK3   And [John the Baptist] preached, saying, There cometh one mightier than I after me, the latchet of whose shoes I am not worthy to stoop down and unloose.[601]

QCMK4   I indeed have baptized you with water: but he shall baptize you with the Holy Ghost.[602]

QCMK5   And immediately the Spirit driveth him into the wilderness.[603]

QCMK6   And he was there in the wilderness forty days, tempted of Satan; and was with the wild beasts; and the angels ministered unto him.[604]

QCMK7   And the scribes which came down from Jerusalem said, He hath Beelzebub, and by the prince of the devils casteth he out devils.[605]

QCMK8   And he called them unto him, and said unto them in parables, How can Satan cast out Satan?[606]

QCMK9 And if a kingdom be divided against itself, that kingdom cannot stand.[607]

QCMK10 And if a house be divided against itself, that house cannot stand.[608]

QCMK11 And if Satan rise up against himself, and be divided, he cannot stand, but hath an end.[609]

QCMK12 No man can enter into a strong man's house, and spoil his goods, except he will first bind the strong man; and then he will spoil his house.[610]

QCMK13 And he said unto them, Is a candle brought to be put under a bushel, or under a bed? and not to be set on a candlestick?[611]

QCMK14 For there is nothing hid, which shall not be manifested; neither was any thing kept secret, but that it should come abroad.[612]

QCMK15 And he said unto them, Take heed what ye hear: with what measure ye mete, it shall be measured to you: and unto you that hear shall more be given.[613]

QCMK16 And he said, Whereunto shall we liken the kingdom of God? or with what comparison shall we compare it?[614]

QCMK17 It is like a grain of mustard seed, which, when it is sown in the earth, is less than all the seeds that be in the earth:[615]

QCMK18 But when it is sown, it groweth up, and becometh greater than all herbs, and shooteth out great branches; so that the fowls of the air may lodge under the shadow of it.[616]

QCMK19 And he called unto him the twelve, and began to send them forth by two and two; and gave them power over unclean spirits;[617]

QCMK20 And commanded them that they should take nothing for their journey, save a staff only; no scrip, no bread, no money in their purse:[618]

QCMK21 But be shod with sandals; and not put on two coats.[619]

QCMK22 And he said unto them, In what place soever ye enter into an house, there abide till ye depart from that place.[620]

QCMK23 And whosoever shall not receive you, nor hear you, when ye depart thence, shake off the dust under your feet for a testimony against them. Verily I say unto you, It shall be more tolerable for Sodom and Gomorrha in the day of judgment, than for that city.[621]

QCMK24 And when he had called the people unto him with his disciples also, he said unto them, Whosoever will come after me, let him deny himself, and take up his cross, and follow me.[622]

QCMK25 Whosoever therefore shall be ashamed of me and of my words in this adulterous and sinful generation; of him also shall the Son of man be ashamed, when he cometh in the glory of his Father with the holy angels.[623]

QCMK26 For every one shall be salted with fire, and every sacrifice shall be salted with salt.[624]

QCMK27 Salt is good: but if the salt have lost his saltness, wherewith will ye season it? Have salt in yourselves, and have peace one with another.[625]

QCMK28 And he said unto them in his doctrine, Beware of the scribes, which love to go in long clothing, and love salutations in the marketplaces,[626]

QCMK29 And the chief seats in the synagogues, and the uppermost rooms at feasts:[627]

QCMK30 Which devour widows' houses, and for a pretence make long prayers: these shall receive greater damnation.[628]

QCMK31 But when they shall lead you, and deliver you up, take no thought beforehand what ye shall speak, neither do ye premeditate: but whatsoever shall be given you in that hour, that speak ye: for it is not ye that speak, but the Holy Ghost.[629]

QCMK32 And then if any man shall say to you, Lo, here is Christ; or, lo, he is there; believe him not:[630]

QCMK33 Take ye heed, watch and pray: for ye know not when the time is.[631]

QCMK34 For the Son of man is as a man taking a far journey, who left his house, and gave authority to his servants, and to every man his work, and commanded the porter to watch.[632]

QCMK35 Watch ye therefore: for ye know not when the master of the house cometh, at even, or at midnight, or at the cockcrowing, or in the morning:[633]

QCMK36 Lest coming suddenly he find you sleeping.[634]

6

Q¹ IN MATTHEW

THE FIRST LAYER OF THE GOSPEL OF Q
Q's Wisdom Teachings of Jesus in Matthew

WRITTEN CIRCA A.D. 30S
88 VERSES FROM THE KING JAMES VERSION[635]

KEY FOR SEABROOK NUMBERING SYSTEM
IN BRIEF: "Q1MT1": Gospel of Q, layer, canonical Gospel, verse.
IN DETAIL: "Q1MT1" means Gospel of Q, layer 1, as found in
Gospel of Matthew (KJV), first verse of layer 1.

Q1MT1 This is the true and original Gospel of the Kingdom as taught by Jesus.[636]

Q1MT2 Blessed are the poor in spirit: for theirs is the kingdom of heaven.[637]

Q1MT3 Blessed are they that mourn: for they shall be comforted.[638]

Q1MT4 Blessed are they which do hunger and thirst after righteousness: for they shall be filled.[639]

Q1MT5 Blessed are ye, when men shall revile you, and persecute you, and shall say all manner of evil against you falsely, for my sake.[640]

Q1MT6 Rejoice, and be exceeding glad: for great is your reward in heaven: for so persecuted they the prophets which were before you.[641]

Q1MT7 Ye are the salt of the earth: but if the salt have lost his savour, wherewith shall it be salted? it is thenceforth good for nothing, but to be cast out, and to be trodden under foot of men.[642]

Q1MT8 But I say unto you, That ye resist not evil: but whosoever shall smite thee on thy right cheek, turn to him the other also.[643]

Q1MT9 And if any man will sue thee at the law, and take away thy coat, let him have thy cloke also.[644]

Q1MT10 Give to him that asketh thee, and from him that would borrow of thee turn not thou away.[645]

Q1MT11 But I say unto you, Love your enemies, bless them that curse you, do good to them that hate you, and pray for them which despitefully use you, and persecute you;[646]

Q1MT12 For if ye love them which love you, what reward have ye? do not even the publicans the same?[647]

Q1MT13 And if ye salute your brethren only, what do ye more than others? do not even the publicans so?[648]

Q1MT14 Be ye therefore perfect, even as your Father which is in heaven is perfect.[649]

Q1MT15 After this manner therefore pray ye: Our Father which art in heaven, Hallowed be thy name.[650]

Q1MT16 Thy kingdom come. Thy will be done in earth, as it is in heaven.[651]

Q1MT17 Give us this day our daily bread.[652]

Q1MT18 And forgive us our debts, as we forgive our debtors.[653]

Q1MT19 And lead us not into temptation, but deliver us from evil: For thine is the kingdom, and the power, and the glory, for ever. Amen.[654]

Q1MT20 Lay not up for yourselves treasures upon earth, where moth and rust doth corrupt, and where thieves break through and steal:[655]

Q1MT21 But lay up for yourselves treasures in heaven, where neither moth nor rust doth corrupt, and where thieves do not break through nor steal:[656]

Q1MT22 For where your treasure is, there will your heart be also.[657]

Q1MT23 Therefore I say unto you, Take no thought for your life, what ye shall eat, or what ye shall drink; nor yet for your body, what ye shall put on. Is not the life more than meat, and the body than raiment?[658]

Q1MT24 Behold the fowls of the air: for they sow not, neither do they reap, nor gather into barns; yet your heavenly Father feedeth them. Are ye not much better than they?[659]

Q1MT25 Which of you by taking thought can add one cubit unto his stature?[660]

Q1MT26 And why take ye thought for raiment? Consider the lilies of the field, how they grow; they toil not, neither do they spin:[661]

Q1MT27 And yet I say unto you, That even Solomon in all his glory was not arrayed like one of these.[662]

Q1MT28 Wherefore, if God so clothe the grass of the field, which to day is, and to morrow is cast into the oven, shall he not much more clothe you, O ye of little faith?[663]

Q1MT29 Therefore take no thought, saying, What shall we eat? or, What shall we drink? or, Wherewithal shall we be clothed?[664]

Q1MT30 (For after all these things do the Gentiles seek:) for your heavenly Father knoweth that ye have need of all these things.[665]

Q1MT31 But seek ye first the kingdom of God, and his righteousness; and all these things shall be added unto you.[666]

Q1MT32 Judge not, that ye be not judged.[667]

Q1MT33 For with what judgment ye judge, ye shall be judged: and with what measure ye mete, it shall be measured to you again.[668]

Q1MT34 And why beholdest thou the mote that is in thy brother's eye, but considerest not the beam that is in thine own eye?[669]

Q1MT35 Or how wilt thou say to thy brother, Let me pull out the mote out of thine eye; and, behold, a beam is in thine own eye?[670]

Q1MT36 Thou hypocrite, first cast out the beam out of thine own eye; and then shalt thou see clearly to cast out the mote out of thy brother's eye.[671]

Q1MT37 Ask, and it shall be given you; seek, and ye shall find; knock, and it shall be opened unto you:[672]

Q1MT38 For every one that asketh receiveth; and he that seeketh findeth; and to him that knocketh it shall be opened.[673]

Q1MT39 Or what man is there of you, whom if his son ask bread, will he give him a stone?[674]

Q1MT40 If ye then, being evil, know how to give good gifts unto your children, how much more shall your Father which is in heaven give good things to them that ask him?[675]

Q1MT41 Therefore all things whatsoever ye would that men should do to you, do ye even so to them: for this is the law and the prophets.[676]

Q1MT42 Ye shall know them by their fruits. Do men gather grapes of thorns, or figs of thistles?[677]

Q1MT43 A good tree cannot bring forth evil fruit, neither can a corrupt tree bring forth good fruit.[678]

Q1MT44 Not every one that saith unto me, Lord, Lord, shall enter into the kingdom of heaven; but he that doeth the will of my Father which is in heaven.[679]

Q1MT45 Therefore whosoever heareth these sayings of mine, and doeth them, I will liken him unto a wise man, which built his house upon a rock:[680]

Q1MT46 And the rain descended, and the floods came, and the winds blew, and beat upon that house; and it fell not: for it was founded upon a rock.[681]

Q1MT47 And every one that heareth these sayings of mine, and doeth them not, shall be likened unto a foolish man, which built his house upon the sand:[682]

Q1MT48 And the rain descended, and the floods came, and the winds blew, and beat upon that house; and it fell: and great was the fall of it.[683]

Q1MT49 And a certain scribe came, and said unto him, Master, I will follow thee whithersoever thou goest.[684]

Q1MT50 And Jesus saith unto him, The foxes have holes, and the birds of the air have nests; but the Son of man hath not where to lay his head.[685]

Q1MT51 And another of his disciples said unto him, Lord, suffer me first to go and bury my father.[686]

Q1MT52 But Jesus said unto him, Follow me; and let the dead bury their dead.[687]

Q1MT53 Then saith he unto his disciples, The harvest truly is plenteous, but the labourers are few;[688]

Q1MT54 Pray ye therefore the Lord of the harvest, that he will send forth labourers into his harvest.[689]

Q1MT55 And as ye go, preach, saying, The kingdom of heaven is at hand.[690]

Q1MT56 Heal the sick, cleanse the lepers, raise the dead, cast out devils: freely ye have received, freely give.[691]

Q1MT57 Provide neither gold, nor silver, nor brass in your purses,[692]

Q1MT58 Nor scrip for your journey, neither two coats, neither shoes, nor yet staves: for the workman is worthy of his meat.[693]

Q1MT59 And when ye come into an house, salute it.[694]

Q1MT60 And if the house be worthy, let your peace come upon it: but if it be not worthy, let your peace return to you.[695]

Q1MT61 And whosoever shall not receive you, nor hear your

words, when ye depart out of that house or city, shake off the dust of your feet.[696]

Q1MT62 Behold, I send you forth as sheep in the midst of wolves: be ye therefore wise as serpents, and harmless as doves.[697]

Q1MT63 The disciple is not above his master, nor the servant above his lord.[698]

Q1MT64 Fear them [Jesus' critics] not therefore: for there is nothing covered, that shall not be revealed; and hid, that shall not be known.[699]

Q1MT65 What I tell you in darkness, that speak ye in light: and what ye hear in the ear, that preach ye upon the housetops.[700]

Q1MT66 And fear not them which kill the body, but are not able to kill the soul: but rather fear him which is able to destroy both soul and body in hell.[701]

Q1MT67 Are not two sparrows sold for a farthing? and one of them shall not fall on the ground without your Father.[702]

Q1MT68 But the very hairs of your head are all numbered.[703]

Q1MT69 Fear ye not therefore, ye are of more value than many sparrows.[704]

Q1MT70 He that loveth father or mother more than me is not worthy of me: and he that loveth son or daughter more than me is not worthy of me.[705]

Q1MT71 And he that taketh not his cross, and followeth after me, is not worthy of me.[706]

Q1MT72 O generation of vipers, how can ye, being evil, speak good things? for out of the abundance of the heart the mouth speaketh.[707]

Q1MT73 A good man out of the good treasure of the heart bringeth forth good things: and an evil man out of the evil treasure bringeth forth evil things.[708]

Q1MT74 Another parable put he forth unto them, saying, The kingdom of heaven is like to a grain of mustard seed, which a man took, and sowed in his field:[709]

Q1MT75 Which indeed is the least of all seeds: but when it is grown, it is the greatest among herbs, and becometh a tree, so that the birds of the air come and lodge in the branches thereof.[710]

Q1MT76 Another parable spake he unto them; The kingdom of heaven is like unto leaven, which a woman took, and hid in three measures of meal, till the whole was leavened.[711]

Q1MT77 Let them [the Pharisees] alone: they be blind leaders of the blind. And if the blind lead the blind, both shall fall into the ditch.[712]

Q1MT78 And Jesus answered and spake unto them again by parables, and said,[713]

Q1MT79 The kingdom of heaven is like unto a certain king, which made a marriage for his son,[714]

Q1MT80 And sent forth his servants to call them that were bidden to the wedding: and they would not come.[715]

Q1MT81 Again, he sent forth other servants, saying, Tell them which are bidden, Behold, I have prepared my dinner: my oxen and my fatlings are killed, and all things are ready: come unto the marriage.[716]

Q1MT82 But they made light of it, and went their ways, one to his farm, another to his merchandise:[717]

Q1MT83 And the remnant took his servants, and entreated them spitefully, and slew them.[718]

Q1MT84 But when the king heard thereof, he was wroth: and he sent forth his armies, and destroyed those murderers, and burned up their city.[719]

Q1MT85 Then saith he to his servants, The wedding is ready, but they which were bidden were not worthy.[720]

Q1MT86 Go ye therefore into the highways, and as many as ye shall find, bid to the marriage.[721]

Q1MT87 So those servants went out into the highways, and gathered together all as many as they found, both bad and good: and the wedding was furnished with guests.[722]

Q1MT88 And whosoever shall exalt himself shall be abased; and he that shall humble himself shall be exalted.[723]

7

Q^6 IN MATTHEW

Q^1, Q^2, AND Q^3 COMBINED
The Complete Gospel of Q in Matthew

WRITTEN CIRCA A.D. 30S-75
246 VERSES FROM THE KING JAMES VERSION[724]

KEY FOR SEABROOK NUMBERING SYSTEM
IN BRIEF: "QCMT1": Gospel of Q, canonical Gospel, verse.
IN DETAIL: "QCMT1" means Gospel of Q, complete, as found in
　　　　　Gospel of Matthew (KJV), first verse of complete
　　　　　edition.

QCMT1　This is part of the true and original Gospel of the Kingdom as taught by Jesus.[725]

QCMT2　But when he [John the Baptist] saw many of the Pharisees and Sadducees come to his baptism, he said unto them, O generation of vipers, who hath warned you to flee from the wrath to come?[726]

QCMT3　Bring forth therefore fruits meet for repentance:[727]

QCMT4　And think not to say within yourselves, We have Abraham to our father: for I say unto you, that God is able of these stones to raise up children unto Abraham.[728]

QCMT5　And now also the axe is laid unto the root of the trees: therefore every tree which bringeth not forth good fruit is hewn down, and cast into the fire.[729]

QCMT6　I indeed baptize you with water unto repentance: but he that cometh after me is mightier than I, whose shoes I am not worthy to bear: he shall baptize you with the Holy Ghost, and with fire:[730]

QCMT7 Whose fan is in his hand, and he will throughly purge his floor, and gather his wheat into the garner; but he will burn up the chaff with unquenchable fire.[731]

QCMT8 Then was Jesus led up of the Spirit into the wilderness to be tempted of the devil.[732]

QCMT9 And when he had fasted forty days and forty nights, he was afterward an hungred.[733]

QCMT10 And when the tempter came to him, he said, If thou be the Son of God, command that these stones be made bread.[734]

QCMT11 But he answered and said, It is written, Man shall not live by bread alone, but by every word that proceedeth out of the mouth of God.[735]

QCMT12 Then the devil taketh him up into the holy city, and setteth him on a pinnacle of the temple,[736]

QCMT13 And saith unto him, If thou be the Son of God, cast thyself down: for it is written, He shall give his angels charge concerning thee: and in their hands they shall bear thee up, lest at any time thou dash thy foot against a stone.[737]

QCMT14 Jesus said unto him, It is written again, Thou shalt not tempt the Lord thy God.[738]

QCMT15 Again, the devil taketh him up into an exceeding high mountain, and sheweth him all the kingdoms of the world, and the glory of them;[739]

QCMT16 And saith unto him, All these things will I give thee, if thou wilt fall down and worship me.[740]

QCMT17 Then saith Jesus unto him, Get thee hence, Satan: for it is written, Thou shalt worship the Lord thy God, and him only shalt thou serve.[741]

QCMT18 Then the devil leaveth him, and, behold, angels came and ministered unto him.[742]

QCMT19 [And Jesus taught the multitudes thusly:] Blessed are the poor in spirit: for theirs is the kingdom of heaven.[743]

QCMT20   Blessed are they that mourn: for they shall be comforted.[744]

QCMT21   Blessed are they which do hunger and thirst after righteousness: for they shall be filled.[745]

QCMT22 Blessed are ye, when men shall revile you, and persecute you, and shall say all manner of evil against you falsely, for my sake.[746]

QCMT23 Rejoice, and be exceeding glad: for great is your reward in heaven: for so persecuted they the prophets which were before you.[747]

QCMT24 Ye are the salt of the earth: but if the salt have lost his savour, wherewith shall it be salted? it is thenceforth good for nothing, but to be cast out, and to be trodden under foot of men.[748]

QCMT25 Neither do men light a candle, and put it under a bushel, but on a candlestick; and it giveth light unto all that are in the house.[749]

QCMT26 For verily I say unto you, Till heaven and earth pass, one jot or one tittle shall in no wise pass from the law, till all be fulfilled.[750]

QCMT27 Agree with thine adversary quickly, whiles thou art in the way with him; lest at any time the adversary deliver thee to the judge, and the judge deliver thee to the officer, and thou be cast into prison.[751]

QCMT28 Verily I say unto thee, Thou shalt by no means come out thence, till thou hast paid the uttermost farthing.[752]

QCMT29 But I say unto you, That whosoever shall put away his wife, saving for the cause of fornication, causeth her to commit adultery: and whosoever shall marry her that is divorced committeth adultery.[753]

QCMT30 But I say unto you, That ye resist not evil: but whosoever shall smite thee on thy right cheek, turn to him the other also.[754]

QCMT31 And if any man will sue thee at the law, and take away thy coat, let him have thy cloke also.[755]

QCMT32 Give to him that asketh thee, and from him that would borrow of thee turn not thou away.[756]

QCMT33 But I say unto you, Love your enemies, bless them that curse you, do good to them that hate you, and pray for them which despitefully use you, and persecute you;[757]

QCMT34 That ye may be the children of your Father which is in heaven: for he maketh his sun to rise on the evil and on the good, and sendeth rain on the just and on the unjust.[758]

QCMT35 For if ye love them which love you, what reward have ye? do not even the publicans the same?[759]

QCMT36 And if ye salute your brethren only, what do ye more than others? do not even the publicans so?[760]

QCMT37 Be ye therefore perfect, even as your Father which is in heaven is perfect.[761]

QCMT38 After this manner therefore pray ye: Our Father which art in heaven, Hallowed be thy name.[762]

QCMT39 Thy kingdom come. Thy will be done in earth, as it is in heaven.[763]

QCMT40 Give us this day our daily bread.[764]

QCMT41 And forgive us our debts, as we forgive our debtors. [765]

QCMT42 And lead us not into temptation, but deliver us from evil: For thine is the kingdom, and the power, and the glory, for ever. Amen. [766]

QCMT43 Lay not up for yourselves treasures upon earth, where moth and rust doth corrupt, and where thieves break through and steal: [767]

QCMT44 But lay up for yourselves treasures in heaven, where neither moth nor rust doth corrupt, and where thieves do not break through nor steal: [768]

QCMT45 For where your treasure is, there will your heart be also. [769]

QCMT46 The light of the body is the eye: if therefore thine eye be single, thy whole body shall be full of light. [770]

QCMT47 But if thine eye be evil, thy whole body shall be full of darkness. If therefore the light that is in thee be darkness, how great is that darkness! [771]

QCMT48 No man can serve two masters: for either he will hate the one, and love the other; or else he will hold to the one, and despise the other. Ye cannot serve God and mammon. [772]

QCMT49 Therefore I say unto you, Take no thought for your life, what ye shall eat, or what ye shall drink; nor yet for your body, what ye shall put on. Is not the life more than meat, and the body than raiment? [773]

QCMT50 Behold the fowls of the air: for they sow not, neither do they reap, nor gather into barns; yet your heavenly Father feedeth them. Are ye not much better than they? [774]

QCMT51 Which of you by taking thought can add one cubit unto his stature? [775]

QCMT52 And why take ye thought for raiment? Consider the lilies of the field, how they grow; they toil not, neither do they spin: [776]

QCMT53 And yet I say unto you, That even Solomon in all his glory was not arrayed like one of these. [777]

QCMT54 Wherefore, if God so clothe the grass of the field, which to day is, and to morrow is cast into the oven, shall he not much more clothe you, O ye of little faith? [778]

QCMT55 Therefore take no thought, saying, What shall we eat? or, What shall we drink? or, Wherewithal shall we be clothed? [779]

QCMT56 (For after all these things do the Gentiles seek:) for your heavenly Father knoweth that ye have need of all these things. [780]

QCMT57 But seek ye first the kingdom of God, and his

righteousness; and all these things shall be added unto you.[781]

QCMT58 Judge not, that ye be not judged.[782]

QCMT59 For with what judgment ye judge, ye shall be judged: and with what measure ye mete, it shall be measured to you again.[783]

QCMT60 And why beholdest thou the mote that is in thy brother's eye, but considerest not the beam that is in thine own eye?[784]

QCMT61 Or how wilt thou say to thy brother, Let me pull out the mote out of thine eye; and, behold, a beam is in thine own eye?[785]

QCMT62 Thou hypocrite, first cast out the beam out of thine own eye; and then shalt thou see clearly to cast out the mote out of thy brother's eye.[786]

QCMT63 Ask, and it shall be given you; seek, and ye shall find; knock, and it shall be opened unto you:[787]

QCMT64 For every one that asketh receiveth; and he that seeketh findeth; and to him that knocketh it shall be opened.[788]

QCMT65 Or what man is there of you, whom if his son ask bread, will he give him a stone?[789]

QCMT66 Or if he ask a fish, will he give him a serpent?[790]

QCMT67 If ye then, being evil, know how to give good gifts unto your children, how much more shall your Father which is in heaven give good things to them that ask him?[791]

QCMT68 Therefore all things whatsoever ye would that men should do to you, do ye even so to them: for this is the law and the prophets.[792]

QCMT69 Enter ye in at the strait gate: for wide is the gate, and broad is the way, that leadeth to destruction, and many there be which go in thereat:[793]

QCMT70 Because strait is the gate, and narrow is the way, which leadeth unto life, and few there be that find it.[794]

QCMT71 Ye shall know them by their fruits. Do men gather grapes of thorns, or figs of thistles?[795]

QCMT72 Even so every good tree bringeth forth good fruit; but a corrupt tree bringeth forth evil fruit.[796]

QCMT73 A good tree cannot bring forth evil fruit, neither can a corrupt tree bring forth good fruit.[797]

QCMT74 Not every one that saith unto me, Lord, Lord, shall enter into the kingdom of heaven; but he that doeth the will of my Father which is in heaven.[798]

QCMT75 Many will say to me in that day, Lord, Lord, have we not prophesied in thy name? and in thy name have cast out devils? and in thy name done many wonderful works?[799]

QCMT76 And then will I profess unto them, I never knew you: depart from me, ye that work iniquity.[800]

QCMT77 Therefore whosoever heareth these sayings of mine, and doeth them, I will liken him unto a wise man, which built his house upon a rock:[801]

QCMT78 And the rain descended, and the floods came, and the winds blew, and beat upon that house; and it fell not: for it was founded upon a rock.[802]

QCMT79 And every one that heareth these sayings of mine, and doeth them not, shall be likened unto a foolish man, which built his house upon the sand:[803]

QCMT80 And the rain descended, and the floods came, and the winds blew, and beat upon that house; and it fell: and great was the fall of it.[804]

QCMT81 And when Jesus was entered into Capernaum, there came unto him a centurion, beseeching him,[805]

QCMT82 And saying, Lord, my servant lieth at home sick of the palsy, grievously tormented.[806]

QCMT83 And Jesus saith unto him, I will come and heal him.[807]

QCMT84 The centurion answered and said, Lord, I am not worthy that thou shouldest come under my roof: but speak the word only, and my servant shall be healed.[808]

QCMT85 For I am a man under authority, having soldiers under me: and I say to this man, Go, and he goeth; and to another, Come, and he cometh; and to my servant, Do this, and he doeth it.[809]

QCMT86 When Jesus heard it, he marvelled, and said to them that followed, Verily I say unto you, I have not found so great faith, no, not in Israel.[810]

QCMT87 And I say unto you, That many shall come from the east and west, and shall sit down with Abraham, and Isaac, and Jacob, in the kingdom of heaven.[811]

QCMT88 But the children of the kingdom shall be cast out into outer darkness: there shall be weeping and gnashing of teeth.[812]

QCMT89 And Jesus said unto the centurion, Go thy way; and as thou hast believed, so be it done unto thee. And his servant was healed in the selfsame hour.[813]

QCMT90 And a certain scribe came, and said unto him, Master,

I will follow thee whithersoever thou goest.[814]

QCMT91 And Jesus saith unto him, The foxes have holes, and the birds of the air have nests; but the Son of man hath not where to lay his head.[815]

QCMT92 And another of his disciples said unto him, Lord, suffer me first to go and bury my father.[816]

QCMT93 But Jesus said unto him, Follow me; and let the dead bury their dead.[817]

QCMT94 Then saith he unto his disciples, The harvest truly is plenteous, but the labourers are few;[818]

QCMT95 Pray ye therefore the Lord of the harvest, that he will send forth labourers into his harvest.[819]

QCMT96 [To the Twelve Apostles Jesus said:] And as ye go, preach, saying, The kingdom of heaven is at hand.[820]

QCMT97 Heal the sick, cleanse the lepers, raise the dead, cast out devils: freely ye have received, freely give.[821]

QCMT98 Provide neither gold, nor silver, nor brass in your purses,[822]

QCMT99 Nor scrip for your journey, neither two coats, neither shoes, nor yet staves: for the workman is worthy of his meat.[823]

QCMT100 And into whatsoever city or town ye shall enter, enquire who in it is worthy; and there abide till ye go thence.[824]

QCMT101 And when ye come into an house, salute it.[825]

QCMT102 And if the house be worthy, let your peace come upon it: but if it be not worthy, let your peace return to you.[826]

QCMT103 And whosoever shall not receive you, nor hear your words, when ye depart out of that house or city, shake off the dust of your feet.[827]

QCMT104 Verily I say unto you, It shall be more tolerable for the land of Sodom and Gomorrha in the day of judgment, than for that city.[828]

QCMT105 Behold, I send you forth as sheep in the midst of wolves: be ye therefore wise as serpents, and harmless as doves.[829]

QCMT106 The disciple is not above his master, nor the servant above his lord.[830]

QCMT107 It is enough for the disciple that he be as his master, and the servant as his lord. If they have called the master of the house Beelzebub, how much more shall they call them of his household?[831]

QCMT108 Fear them not therefore: for there is nothing covered, that shall not be revealed; and hid, that shall not be known.[832]

QCMT109 What I tell you in darkness, that speak ye in light: and what ye hear in the ear, that preach ye upon the housetops.[833]

QCMT110 And fear not them which kill the body, but are not able to kill the soul: but rather fear him which is able to destroy both soul and body in hell.[834]

QCMT111 Are not two sparrows sold for a farthing? and one of them shall not fall on the ground without your Father.[835]

QCMT112 But the very hairs of your head are all numbered.[836]

QCMT113 Fear ye not therefore, ye are of more value than many sparrows.[837]

QCMT114 Whosoever therefore shall confess me before men, him will I confess also before my Father which is in heaven.[838]

QCMT115 But whosoever shall deny me before men, him will I also deny before my Father which is in heaven.[839]

QCMT116 Think not that I am come to send peace on earth: I came not to send peace, but a sword.[840]

QCMT117 For I am come to set a man at variance against his father, and the daughter against her mother, and the daughter in law against her mother in law.[841]

QCMT118 And a man's foes shall be they of his own household.[842]

QCMT119 He that loveth father or mother more than me is not worthy of me: and he that loveth son or daughter more than me is not worthy of me.[843]

QCMT120 And he that taketh not his cross, and followeth after me, is not worthy of me.[844]

QCMT121 He that findeth his life shall lose it: and he that loseth his life for my sake shall find it.[845]

QCMT122 He that receiveth you receiveth me, and he that receiveth me receiveth him that sent me.[846]

QCMT123 Now when John [the Baptist] had heard in the prison the works of Christ, he sent two of his disciples,[847]

QCMT124 And said unto him, Art thou he that should come, or do we look for another?[848]

QCMT125 Jesus answered and said unto them, Go and shew John again those things which ye do hear and see:[849]

QCMT126 The blind receive their sight, and the lame walk, the lepers are cleansed, and the deaf hear, the dead are raised up, and the poor have the gospel preached to them.[850]

QCMT127 And blessed is he, whosoever shall not be offended in me.[851]

QCMT128   And as they departed, Jesus began to say unto the multitudes concerning John, What went ye out into the wilderness to see? A reed shaken with the wind?[852]

QCMT129   But what went ye out for to see? A man clothed in soft raiment? behold, they that wear soft clothing are in kings' houses.[853]

QCMT130   But what went ye out for to see? A prophet? yea, I say unto you, and more than a prophet.[854]

QCMT131   For this is he, of whom it is written, Behold, I send my messenger before thy face, which shall prepare thy way before thee.[855]

QCMT132   Verily I say unto you, Among them that are born of women there hath not risen a greater than John the Baptist: notwithstanding he that is least in the kingdom of heaven is greater than he.[856]

QCMT133   And from the days of John the Baptist until now the kingdom of heaven suffereth violence, and the violent take it by force.[857]

QCMT134   For all the prophets and the law prophesied until John.[858]

QCMT135   But whereunto shall I liken this generation? It is like unto children sitting in the markets, and calling unto their fellows,[859]

QCMT136   And saying, We have piped unto you, and ye have not danced; we have mourned unto you, and ye have not lamented.[860]

QCMT137   For John came neither eating nor drinking, and they say, He hath a devil.[861]

QCMT138   The Son of man came eating and drinking, and they say, Behold a man gluttonous, and a winebibber, a friend of publicans and sinners. But wisdom is justified of her children.[862]

QCMT139   Then began he to upbraid the cities wherein most of his mighty works were done, because they repented not:[863]

QCMT140   Woe unto thee, Chorazin! woe unto thee, Bethsaida! for if the mighty works, which were done in you, had been done in Tyre and Sidon, they would have repented long ago in sackcloth and ashes.[864]

QCMT141   But I say unto you, It shall be more tolerable for Tyre and Sidon at the day of judgment, than for you.[865]

QCMT142   And thou, Capernaum, which art exalted unto heaven, shalt be brought down to hell: for if the mighty works, which have been done in thee, had been done in Sodom, it would have remained until this day.[866]

QCMT143   But I say unto you, That it shall be more tolerable for the land of Sodom in the day of judgment, than for thee.[867]

QCMT144 At that time Jesus answered and said, I thank thee, O Father, Lord of heaven and earth, because thou hast hid these things from the wise and prudent, and hast revealed them unto babes.[868]

QCMT145 Even so, Father: for so it seemed good in thy sight.[869]

QCMT146 All things are delivered unto me of my Father: and no man knoweth the Son, but the Father; neither knoweth any man the Father, save the Son, and he to whomsoever the Son will reveal him.[870]

QCMT147 Then was brought unto him one possessed with a devil, blind, and dumb: and he healed him, insomuch that the blind and dumb both spake and saw.[871]

QCMT148 And all the people were amazed, and said, Is not this the son of David?[872]

QCMT149 But when the Pharisees heard it, they said, This fellow doth not cast out devils, but by Beelzebub the prince of the devils.[873]

QCMT150 And Jesus knew their thoughts, and said unto them, Every kingdom divided against itself is brought to desolation; and every city or house divided against itself shall not stand:[874]

QCMT151 And if Satan cast out Satan, he is divided against himself; how shall then his kingdom stand?[875]

QCMT152 And if I by Beelzebub cast out devils, by whom do your children cast them out? therefore they shall be your judges.[876]

QCMT153 But if I cast out devils by the Spirit of God, then the kingdom of God is come unto you.[877]

QCMT154 Or else how can one enter into a strong man's house, and spoil his goods, except he first bind the strong man? and then he will spoil his house.[878]

QCMT155 He that is not with me is against me; and he that gathereth not with me scattereth abroad.[879]

QCMT156 And whosoever speaketh a word against the Son of man, it shall be forgiven him: but whosoever speaketh against the Holy Ghost, it shall not be forgiven him, neither in this world, neither in the world to come.[880]

QCMT157 Either make the tree good, and his fruit good; or else make the tree corrupt, and his fruit corrupt: for the tree is known by his fruit.[881]

QCMT158 Then certain of the scribes and of the Pharisees answered, saying, Master, we would see a sign from thee.[882]

QCMT159 But he answered and said unto them, An evil and adulterous generation seeketh after a sign; and there shall no sign be given to it, but the sign of the prophet Jonas:[883]

QCMT160 For as Jonas was three days and three nights in the whale's belly; so shall the Son of man be three days and three nights in the heart of the earth.[884]

QCMT161 The men of Nineveh shall rise in judgment with this generation, and shall condemn it: because they repented at the preaching of Jonas; and, behold, a greater than Jonas is here.[885]

QCMT162 The queen of the south shall rise up in the judgment with this generation, and shall condemn it: for she came from the uttermost parts of the earth to hear the wisdom of Solomon; and, behold, a greater than Solomon is here.[886]

QCMT163 When the unclean spirit is gone out of a man, he walketh through dry places, seeking rest, and findeth none.[887]

QCMT164 Then he saith, I will return into my house from whence I came out; and when he is come, he findeth it empty, swept, and garnished.[888]

QCMT165 Then goeth he, and taketh with himself seven other spirits more wicked than himself, and they enter in and dwell there: and the last state of that man is worse than the first. Even so shall it be also unto this wicked generation.[889]

QCMT166 But blessed are your eyes, for they see: and your ears, for they hear.[890]

QCMT167 For verily I say unto you, That many prophets and righteous men have desired to see those things which ye see, and have not seen them; and to hear those things which ye hear, and have not heard them.[891]

QCMT168 Another parable put he forth unto them, saying, The kingdom of heaven is like to a grain of mustard seed, which a man took, and sowed in his field:[892]

QCMT169 Which indeed is the least of all seeds: but when it is grown, it is the greatest among herbs, and becometh a tree, so that the birds of the air come and lodge in the branches thereof.[893]

QCMT170 Another parable spake he unto them; The kingdom of heaven is like unto leaven, which a woman took, and hid in three measures of meal, till the whole was leavened.[894]

QCMT171 Let them [the Pharisees] alone: they be blind leaders of the blind. And if the blind lead the blind, both shall fall into the ditch.[895]

QCMT172 [When the Pharisees asked Him to show them a miracle] He answered and said unto them, When it is evening, ye say, It will be fair weather: for the sky is red.[896]

QCMT173 And in the morning, It will be foul weather to day: for the sky is red and lowring. O ye hypocrites, ye can discern the face of the sky; but can ye not discern the signs of the times?[897]

QCMT174 And Jesus said unto them, Because of your unbelief: for verily I say unto you, If ye have faith as a grain of mustard seed, ye shall say unto this mountain, Remove hence to yonder place; and it shall remove; and nothing shall be impossible unto you.[898]

QCMT175 But whoso shall offend one of these little ones which believe in me, it were better for him that a millstone were hanged about his neck, and that he were drowned in the depth of the sea.[899]

QCMT176 Woe unto the world because of offences! for it must needs be that offences come; but woe to that man by whom the offence cometh![900]

QCMT177 How think ye? if a man have an hundred sheep, and one of them be gone astray, doth he not leave the ninety and nine, and goeth into the mountains, and seeketh that which is gone astray?[901]

QCMT178 And if so be that he find it, verily I say unto you, he rejoiceth more of that sheep, than of the ninety and nine which went not astray.[902]

QCMT179 Even so it is not the will of your Father which is in heaven, that one of these little ones should perish.[903]

QCMT180 Moreover if thy brother shall trespass against thee, go and tell him his fault between thee and him alone: if he shall hear thee, thou hast gained thy brother.[904]

QCMT181 Then came Peter to him, and said, Lord, how oft shall my brother sin against me, and I forgive him? till seven times?[905]

QCMT182 Jesus saith unto him, I say not unto thee, Until seven times: but, Until seventy times seven.[906]

QCMT183 And Jesus said unto them, Verily I say unto you, That ye which have followed me, in the regeneration when the Son of man shall sit in the throne of his glory, ye also shall sit upon twelve thrones, judging the twelve tribes of Israel.[907]

QCMT184 Whether of them twain did the will of his father? They say unto him, The first. Jesus saith unto them, Verily I say unto you, That the publicans and the harlots go into the kingdom of God before you.[908]

QCMT185 For John came unto you in the way of righteousness, and ye believed him not: but the publicans and the harlots believed him: and ye, when ye had seen it, repented not afterward, that ye might believe him.[909]

QCMT186 The kingdom of heaven is like unto a certain king, which made a marriage for his son,[910]

QCMT187 And sent forth his servants to call them that were bidden to the wedding: and they would not come.[911]

QCMT188 Again, he sent forth other servants, saying, Tell them which are bidden, Behold, I have prepared my dinner: my oxen and my fatlings are killed, and all things are ready: come unto the marriage.[912]

QCMT189 But they made light of it, and went their ways, one to his farm, another to his merchandise:[913]

QCMT190 And the remnant took his servants, and entreated them spitefully, and slew them.[914]

QCMT191 But when the king heard thereof, he was wroth: and he sent forth his armies, and destroyed those murderers, and burned up their city.[915]

QCMT192 Then saith he to his servants, The wedding is ready, but they which were bidden were not worthy.[916]

QCMT193 Go ye therefore into the highways, and as many as ye shall find, bid to the marriage.[917]

QCMT194 So those servants went out into the highways, and gathered together all as many as they found, both bad and good: and the wedding was furnished with guests.[918]

QCMT195 For they [the Pharisees] bind heavy burdens and grievous to be borne, and lay them on men's shoulders; but they themselves will not move them with one of their fingers.[919]

QCMT196 And [they] love the uppermost rooms at feasts, and the chief seats in the synagogues,[920]

QCMT197 And greetings in the markets,[921]

QCMT198 And whosoever shall exalt himself shall be abased; and he that shall humble himself shall be exalted.[922]

QCMT199 But woe unto you, scribes and Pharisees, hypocrites! for ye shut up the kingdom of heaven against men: for ye neither go in yourselves, neither suffer ye them that are entering to go in.[923]

QCMT200 Woe unto you, scribes and Pharisees, hypocrites! for ye pay tithe of mint and anise and cummin, and have omitted the weightier matters of the law, judgment, mercy, and faith: these ought ye to have done, and not to leave the other undone.[924]

QCMT201 Woe unto you, scribes and Pharisees, hypocrites! for ye make clean the outside of the cup and of the platter, but within they are full of extortion and excess.[925]

QCMT202 Thou blind Pharisee, cleanse first that which is within the cup and platter, that the outside of them may be clean also.[926]

QCMT203 Woe unto you, scribes and Pharisees, hypocrites! for ye are like unto whited sepulchres, which indeed appear beautiful outward, but are within full of dead men's bones, and of all uncleanness.[927]

QCMT204 Woe unto you, scribes and Pharisees, hypocrites! because ye build the tombs of the prophets, and garnish the sepulchres of the righteous,[928]

QCMT205 And say, If we had been in the days of our fathers, we would not have been partakers with them in the blood of the prophets.[929]

QCMT206 Wherefore ye be witnesses unto yourselves, that ye are the children of them which killed the prophets.[930]

QCMT207 Wherefore, behold, I send unto you prophets, and wise men, and scribes: and some of them ye shall kill and crucify; and some of them shall ye scourge in your synagogues, and persecute them from city to city:[931]

QCMT208 That upon you may come all the righteous blood shed upon the earth, from the blood of righteous Abel unto the blood of Zacharias son of Barachias, whom ye slew between the temple and the altar.[932]

QCMT209 Verily I say unto you, All these things shall come upon this generation.[933]

QCMT210 O Jerusalem, Jerusalem, thou that killest the prophets, and stonest them which are sent unto thee, how often would I have gathered thy children together, even as a hen gathereth her chickens under her wings, and ye would not![934]

QCMT211 Behold, your house is left unto you desolate.[935]

QCMT212 For I say unto you, Ye shall not see me henceforth, till ye shall say, Blessed is he that cometh in the name of the Lord.[936]

QCMT213 Wherefore if they shall say unto you, Behold, he [the Christ] is in the desert; go not forth: behold, he is in the secret chambers; believe it not.[937]

QCMT214 For as the lightning cometh out of the east, and shineth even unto the west; so shall also the coming of the Son of man be.[938]

QCMT215 For wheresoever the carcase is, there will the eagles be gathered together.[939]

QCMT216 But as the days of Noe [Noah] were, so shall also the coming of the Son of man be.[940]

QCMT217 For as in the days that were before the flood they were eating and drinking, marrying and giving in marriage, until the day that Noe entered into the ark,[941]

QCMT218 And knew not until the flood came, and took them all away; so shall also the coming of the Son of man be.[942]

QCMT219 Then shall two be in the field; the one shall be taken, and the other left.[943]

QCMT220 Two women shall be grinding at the mill; the one shall be taken, and the other left.[944]

QCMT221 But know this, that if the goodman of the house had known in what watch the thief would come, he would have watched, and would not have suffered his house to be broken up.[945]

QCMT222 Therefore be ye also ready: for in such an hour as ye think not the Son of man cometh.[946]

QCMT223 Who then is a faithful and wise servant, whom his lord hath made ruler over his household, to give them meat in due season?[947]

QCMT224 Blessed is that servant, whom his lord when he cometh shall find so doing.[948]

QCMT225 Verily I say unto you, That he shall make him ruler over all his goods.[949]

QCMT226 But and if that evil servant shall say in his heart, My lord delayeth his coming;[950]

QCMT227 And shall begin to smite his fellowservants, and to eat and drink with the drunken;[951]

QCMT228 The lord of that servant shall come in a day when he looketh not for him, and in an hour that he is not aware of,[952]

QCMT229 And shall cut him asunder, and appoint him his portion with the hypocrites: there shall be weeping and gnashing of teeth.[953]

QCMT230 For the kingdom of heaven is as a man travelling into a far country, who called his own servants, and delivered unto them his goods.[954]

QCMT231 And unto one he gave five talents, to another two, and to another one; to every man according to his several ability; and straightway took his journey.[955]

QCMT232 Then he that had received the five talents went and traded with the same, and made them other five talents.[956]

QCMT233 And likewise he that had received two, he also gained other two.[957]

QCMT234 But he that had received one went and digged in the earth, and hid his lord's money.[958]

QCMT235 After a long time the lord of those servants cometh, and reckoneth with them.[959]

QCMT236 And so he that had received five talents came and brought other five talents, saying, Lord, thou deliveredst unto me five talents: behold, I have gained beside them five talents more.[960]

QCMT237 His lord said unto him, Well done, thou good and faithful servant: thou hast been faithful over a few things, I will make thee ruler over many things: enter thou into the joy of thy lord.[961]

QCMT238 He also that had received two talents came and said, Lord, thou deliveredst unto me two talents: behold, I have gained two other talents beside them.[962]

QCMT239 His lord said unto him, Well done, good and faithful servant; thou hast been faithful over a few things, I will make thee ruler over many things: enter thou into the joy of thy lord.[963]

QCMT240 Then he which had received the one talent came and said, Lord, I knew thee that thou art an hard man, reaping where thou hast not sown, and gathering where thou hast not strawed:[964]

QCMT241 And I was afraid, and went and hid thy talent in the earth: lo, there thou hast that is thine.[965]

QCMT242 His lord answered and said unto him, Thou wicked and slothful servant, thou knewest that I reap where I sowed not, and gather where I have not strawed:[966]

QCMT243 Thou oughtest therefore to have put my money to the exchangers, and then at my coming I should have received mine own with usury.[967]

QCMT244 Take therefore the talent from him, and give it unto him which hath ten talents.[968]

QCMT245 For unto every one that hath shall be given, and he shall have abundance: but from him that hath not shall be taken away even that which he hath.[969]

QCMT246 And cast ye the unprofitable servant into outer darkness: there shall be weeping and gnashing of teeth.[970]

NOTES

1. Kloppenborg, QP, p. xxiv.
2. Matthew 4:23; 9:35; 24:14; Mark 1:14.
3. For more on this topic, see Seabrook, JLOA, passim.
4. 1 Corinthians 2:16.
5. See e.g., Matthew 6:33; Mark 1:15; 4:11; Luke 4:43; John 3:3; Acts 1:3.
6. See Harnack, TSOJ, p. 232.
7. John 18:36.
8. Luke 17:21.
9. See my works: *Christ Is All and In All: Rediscovering Your Divine Nature and the Kingdom Within*; *Jesus and the Law of Attraction*; and *The Bible and the Law of Attraction*.
10. Matthew 6:33.
11. See e.g., John 5:19, 30-31, 36, 41, 43; 6:38; 7:14-19, 28-29; 8:28-29, 40, 42, 50, 54; 14:24, 28; 8:50. Paul held the same belief. See 1 Corinthians 4:4.
12. Seabrook, JLOA, p. 413.
13. John 14:20; 17:21. See also Colossians 3:11.
14. 2 Peter 1:4; Hebrews 12:10.
15. John 10:34; 14:12.
16. Kümmel, p. 63. Some believe that in 1880 Eduard Simons was the first to use the designation Q. See e.g., Robinson, Hoffmann, and Kloppenborg, p. 23.
17. See Kümmel, pp. 217-228; Mack, p. 224.
18. In particular are what must be the authentic words of Jesus in John 10:34 regarding the Good News of the doctrine of Theosis, or God in Man. See Seabrook, CIAAIA, passim.
19. For more on this topic, see Seabrook, JLOA, Appendix B.
20. See Crusé, p. 127. In my opinion, as well as the opinion of many others, Papias could have only been referring to the by then "lost" Gospel of Q, though I do not agree with Papias that Matthew was the author. Some postulate that Papias was referring not to Q, but to The Gospel of the Hebrews (see Kloppenborg, EQ, p. 281). See also Hawkins, pp. xiii-xiv; McKenzie, s.v. "Synoptic Question"; Loetscher, s.v. "Gospel and Gospels."
21. For Paul's reference, see Acts 20:35, where he cites a saying by Jesus that is not found in the canonical Bible.
22. See Harnack, TSOJ, pp. 187-192, 251.
23. Luke 1:1.
24. This is my personal calculation.
25. See Mack, p. 259.
26. Harnack explains this fact in this way: "Our Lord during the first and longest period of His ministry did not speak of Himself as the Messiah (because He at first neither regarded Himself as Messiah, nor indeed could so regard Himself) and even rejected the title of Messiahship when it was applied to himself." Harnack, TSOJ, pp. 244-245.
27. Harnack, TSOJ, p. 170.
28. Pertaining to the last item, see Harnack, TSOJ, p. 229.
29. Matthew 5:17.
30. Harnack, TSOJ, p. 235.
31. Harnack, TSOJ, p. 238.
32. Seabrook, JLOA, p. 400.
33. Mish, s.v. "kerygma."
34. Harnack, TSOJ, p. 234.
35. John 1:38, 49; 3:2; 6:25.
36. Luke 17:21.
37. Harnack, TSOJ, p. 168.
38. See Seabrook, JLOA, pp. 421-435.
39. Many continue to debate whether the Lord's Prayer was actually part of Q. My own opinion on this matter is that it was probably *not* contained in Q. Despite this, I have included the Lord's Prayer in my reconstructions of Q since this supposition is now widely accepted.
40. See Seabrook, JLOA, passim.
41. Matthew 4:23; 9:35; 24:14; Mark 1:14.
42. Scholars call individual passages in Q (and other ancient material) *logia* and multiple ones *logion*, or alternately, pericope and pericopae respectively.

43. Matthew 7:24, 26; Luke 6:47; 9:44; John 14:24.

44. Matthew 7:28; 19:1; 26:1; Luke 1:65; 2:51; 7:1; 9:28; John 10:19.

45. Kloppenborg, TFOQ, p. 81. See also Orton, pp. 70-122. Note that Q is currently thought to be comprised of about 240 verses, while Matthew contains 1,071 verses, Mark 278 verses, and Luke 1,151 verses. The New Testament as a whole contains 138,020 verses. Thus calculated specifically by number of verses, Q represents 9.6 percent of the Synoptic Gospels and a mere 0.17 percent of the New Testament.

46. See e.g., Luke 1:1; John 21:25; Acts 1:3.

47. See e.g., Acts 20:35. The majority of ancient documents are replete with missing words, lines, and even paragraphs. Streeter cites the example of certain manuscripts of Homer in which as many as 60 lines have been excised. Streeter, TFG, p. 307.

48. Pertaining to the latter issue, see e.g., Harnack, TSOJ, pp. 117-126.

49. See Loetscher, s.v. "Gospel and Gospels."

50. See Miller, p. 249.

51. Matthew 4:23; 9:35; 24:14; Mark 1:14.

52. Hoeller, p. 186.

53. See e.g., Miller, passim; Barnstone, passim.

54. Harnack, TSOJ, p. 248.

55. Jülicher, AITTNT, p. 359.

56. See Loetscher, s.v. "Gospel and Gospels"; Kümmel, p. 67; Harnack, TSOJ, pp. 115-116, 247-248.

57. Streeter, TFG, p. xiii.

58. Harnack, CAH, p. 57.

59. Harnack, TSOJ, p. 250.

60. Jülicher, AITTNT, p. 358.

61. Harnack, TSOJ, pp. 227-228.

62. Harnack, TSOJ, p. x. See also pp. 116, 185, 202, 211. Jülicher made reference to Q[1] several years earlier than Harnack. See Jülicher, AITTNT, p. 604.

63. Matthew 4:23; 9:35; 24:14; Mark 1:14.

64. See Luke 21:32; 1 Thessalonians 4:16-17. Mystical Christians, as just one example, believe that the "Second Coming" does not refer to Jesus' literal physical return, but rather to an inner transformation of consciousness in each individual, brought on by the Indwelling Christ which exists within every person (John 1:9; Colossians 3:11). For more on this important subject, see my books: *Christ Is All and In All*, *Jesus and the Law of Attraction*, and *The Bible and the Law of Attraction*.

65. See Hooke, passim; Graves and Patai, passim; Patai, passim; Graves, TGM, passim; Walker, passim; Campbell, passim; J. M. Robertson, PC, passim; J. M. Robertson, CAM, passim; Weigall, passim; Hoeller, p. 46.

66. Sophia is the Greek word for "wisdom."

67. See e.g., Q2LK64 (Luke 11:49).

68. Kümmel, p. 76.

69. Kümmel, p. 86; Hawkins, pp. 93-122.

70. See Kümmel, pp. 47, 70; Kloppenborg, TFOQ, p. 9.

71. All of these elements can be found in the "biographies" of untold numbers of pre-Christian Pagan and Jewish heroes, saints, leaders, and deities. See e.g., Enslin, p. 157; J. M. Robertson, PC, passim; Weigall, passim. Note: The last twelve verses of the last chapter of Mark, (16:9-20), which contain the overtly Paganistic Resurrection account, is fraudulent, a late interpolation (2nd Century) that was understandably not declared "canonical" until the year 1545. Seabrook, JLOA, p. 519. For a full discussion on this topic, see Streeter, TFG, pp. 333-360.

72. Jackson, pp. 18, 25.

73. For a list of worldwide sacrificial saviors, see Seabrook, CBC, pp. 80-81.

74. See e.g., Mark 1:1; 3:11; 15:39. See also Harnack, TSOJ, p. 167.

75. For more on this topic, see Mack, pp. 2-3, 172, 178-180. Though Mark was certainly instrumental in sculpting the figure and biography of Jesus as found in the New Testament, I cannot agree with Bruno Bauer who, in 1840, declared that Jesus was a wholly fictitious character created by Mark. See J. M. Robertson, p. 5.

76. Harnack, TSOJ, pp. 249-250.

77. It has been suggested that Matthew altered Mark, in part, in order to rid the Marcan text of scriptures that showed, for example, discourtesy toward Jesus (Mark 4:38; 10:18) and criticism of the Apostles (Mark 10:35). Luke did the same. For example, compare Mark 4:38 with Luke 8:24. See Metzger and Coogan, s.v. "Synoptic Problem"; Butler, s.v. "Harmony of the Gospels."

78. See Kümmel, pp. 69-70; Mack, p. 3.

79. See e.g., Butler, s.v. "Q"; Livingstone and Cross, s.v. "Q"; Miller, p. 249; Kümmel, p. 69; Harnack, TSOJ, pp. xii, 38-39, 112-113; Streeter, TFG, pp. 271, 275, 285; Kloppenborg, TFOQ, pp. 41, 64, 69-80; Kloppenborg, QP, p. xxx; Mack, p. 22.

80. In the minds of the Q people, once Q was absorbed into Matthew, Luke, and Mark (not to mention numerous other noncanonical Gospels and works), they probably saw little reason to preserve it. Thus, it gradually fell out of use and eventually vanished. After all, it was considered a theological document, not a historical one. At the time then, little or no importance was attached to it.

81. The Gospel of Thomas (and its 114 sayings, or doctrines, of Jesus) was discovered at Nag Hammadi, Egypt, in 1945, with the first English translation coming out in 1959. This particular (physical) document has been dated to around the year A.D. 340, although earlier corroborating finds at Oxyrhynchus, Egypt, date back to at least A.D. 130. Due to the style, wording, and tone of The Gospel of Thomas, the Nag Hammadi and Oxyrhynchus fragments must have been based on a scroll containing the core sayings of Jesus that was composed as early as the 30s or 40s A.D.—in other words, The Gospel of Q. Thus, the original Gospel of Thomas was probably written sometime between A.D. 50 and 75. This makes The Gospel of Thomas—which may actually turn out to be a version of The Gospel of Q—of particular importance to those who are interested in learning about the pre-Paganized, pre-apotheosized, pre-politicized, pre-mythologized, pre-Catholicized figure of Jesus, His original teachings, and His original followers, the Jesus community of Q.

82. Mack, p. 181.

83. See Hoeller, p. 186.

84. Harnack, TSOJ, pp. 250-251.

85. See Mack, pp. 172, 177-180, passim.

86. See e.g., Matthew 12:41-42; 23:36; 24:34; Mark 8:12; 13:30; Luke 7:31; 11:30-32, 50; 17:25; 21:32.

87. See John 18:36.

88. It should be noted here that while many Q scholars exclude Luke 17:20-21 (see e.g., Mack, p. 261; Kloppenborg, QP, p. 188), a few include these two scriptures (see e.g., Kloppenborg, QP, pp. 188-189). I belong to the latter category, which is why both appear in my reconstructions of Q2LK and QCLK.

89. For more on the mystical Christian doctrine of the "Kingdom Within," see Seabrook, JLOA, passim; Seabrook, BLOA, passim; Seabrook, CIAAIA, passim.

90. Kümmel, pp. 63, 69-70.

91. See Kümmel, pp. 55-56; Loetscher, s.v. "Gospel and Gospels."

92. Crusé, p. 127.

93. See J. M. Robertson, PC, passim; Weigall, passim.

94. For more on the Church's Paganization process, see Dowley, pp. 300-301.

95. At the same time it must be admitted that the four Evangelists were not historians and never meant the canonical Gospels to be viewed as historical documents. They were not even authors in the strict sense of the word. Rather, as is clear from comparing Q¹ and The Gospel of Thomas with the canonical Gospels, they were editors, anthologists, revisors, censors, amenders, emenders, propagandists, redactors, mythographers, and mythologists. The countless contradictions, conflicting theological interpretations, and differing scriptural order, inclusions, and exclusions between the four Gospels is but one proof of these facts.

96. Seabrook, JLOA, p. 400.

97. Hoeller, p. 43.

98. Seabrook, CIAAIA, p. 76.

99. Cross and Livingstone, s.v. "Mary, the Blessed Virgin"; Dowley, p. 183.

100. Cross and Livingston, s.v. "Mary, the Blessed Virgin."

101. Dowley, p. 513.

102. Seabrook, JLOA, p. 521.

103. James 1:27.

104. Seabrook, JLOA, p. 521. It is clear to anyone familiar with Paul's letters that he was completely unaware of such things as Jesus' virgin birth, His baptism by John, the Twelve Apostles, etc. He is oblivious to even the primary tenets and stories of the Gospels. He cites only one quote of Jesus (1 Corinthians 11:23-25), which is an obvious interpolation. Paul's Jesus is not the well-known Christ of Matthew, Mark, Luke, and John, but rather the mystical sacrificed and resurrected solar-god of Paganism (identical to Helios, Apollo, Ra, Phoebus, Sol, etc.), which is why Emperor Constantine later equated Jesus with the rising and dying Pagan god Sol Invictus. The only logical explanation for Paul's silence is that Jesus had not been Paganized, mythologized, and deified at the time Paul was writing—that is, the ancient Judeo-Pagan Passion Play had not yet been appended to the life story of our Lord. Either that or Paul did know of these things, but for some reason did not consider them pertinent or important. Either way, these facts continue to haunt the institutionalized Christian Church. For more on this topic, see Seabrook, CBC, pp. 29, 37, 65, 121; Wells, pp. 22-25; J. M. Robertson, PC, pp. 67-69; Graham, pp. 409-421;

Weigall, passim.
105. Kümmel, pp. 71, 73-74.
106. See Enslin, pp. 154-155; J. M. Robertson, CAM, passim.
107. Harnack, TSOJ, p. 171.
108. Matthew 13:55; Mark 6:3; Luke 3:23; 4:22; John 1:45; 6:42; Galatians 4:4. According to a recently discovered text known as the "Slavonic Josephus" (which is probably a copy of the original unedited version of the great historian's works), Jesus was an ordinary though God-realized man. See Baigent, Leigh, and Lincoln, pp. 377-378; Eisler, pp. 167, 427.
109. See Seabrook, CIAAIA, passim.
110. Kümmel, p. 72.
111. Harnack, TSOJ, p. vi.
112. Sources for Q1LK: Lochlainn Seabrook; Harnack, TSOJ, pp. 127-146; Kloppenborg, TFOQ, pp. 342-345.
113. My hypothetical reconstruction of Q1LK's missing incipit (Q1LK1). As such, though it is counted as a passage here in Q1LK, it does not appear in and is not counted as part of QCLK. (BEGINNING OF Q¹ IN LUKE.)
114. Luke 6:20b (Q1LK2).
115. Luke 6:21 (Q1LK3).
116. Luke 6:22 (Q1LK4).
117. Luke 6:23b (Q1LK5).
118. Luke 6:27 (Q1LK6).
119. Luke 6:28 (Q1LK7).
120. Luke 6:29 (Q1LK8).
121. Luke 6:30 (Q1LK9).
122. Luke 6:31 (Q1LK10).
123. Luke 6:32 (Q1LK11).
124. Luke 6:33 (Q1LK12).
125. Luke 6:34 (Q1LK13).
126. Luke 6:35 (Q1LK14).
127. Luke 6:36 (Q1LK15).
128. Luke 6:37 (Q1LK16).
129. Luke 6:38 (Q1LK17).
130. Luke 6:39 (Q1LK18).
131. Luke 6:40 (Q1LK19).
132. Luke 6:41 (Q1LK20).
133. Luke 6:42 (Q1LK21).
134. Luke 6:43 (Q1LK22).
135. Luke 6:44 (Q1LK23).
136. Luke 6:45 (Q1LK24).
137. Luke 6:46 (Q1LK25).
138. Luke 6:47 (Q1LK26).
139. Luke 6:48 (Q1LK27).
140. Luke 6:49 (Q1LK28).
141. Luke 9:57 (Q1LK29).
142. Luke 9:58 (Q1LK30).
143. Luke 9:59 (Q1LK31).
144. Luke 9:60 (Q1LK32).
145. Luke 9:61 (Q1LK33).
146. Luke 9:62 (Q1LK34).
147. Luke 10:2 (Q1LK35).
148. Luke 10:3 (Q1LK36).
149. Luke 10:4 (Q1LK37).
150. Luke 10:5 (Q1LK38).
151. Luke 10:6 (Q1LK39).
152. Luke 10:7 (Q1LK40).
153. Luke 10:8 (Q1LK41).
154. Luke 10:9 (Q1LK42).
155. Luke 10:10 (Q1LK43).
156. Luke 10:11 (Q1LK44).

157. Luke 10:16 (Q1LK45).
158. Luke 11:2 (Q1LK46).
159. Luke 11:3 (Q1LK47).
160. Luke 11:4 (Q1LK48).
161. Luke 11:9 (Q1LK49).
162. Luke 11:10 (Q1LK50).
163. Luke 11:11 (Q1LK51).
164. Luke 11:12 (Q1LK52).
165. Luke 11:13 (Q1LK53).
166. Luke 12:2 (Q1LK54).
167. Luke 12:3 (Q1LK55).
168. Luke 12:4 (Q1LK56).
169. Luke 12:5 (Q1LK57).
170. Luke 12:6 (Q1LK58).
171. Luke 12:7 (Q1LK59).
172. Luke 12:11 (Q1LK60).
173. Luke 12:12 (Q1LK61).
174. Luke 12:22b (Q1LK62).
175. Luke 12:23 (Q1LK63).
176. Luke 12:24 (Q1LK64).
177. Luke 12:25 (Q1LK65).
178. Luke 12:26 (Q1LK66).
179. Luke 12:27 (Q1LK67).
180. Luke 12:28 (Q1LK68).
181. Luke 12:29 (Q1LK69).
182. Luke 12:30 (Q1LK70).
183. Luke 12:31 (Q1LK71).
184. Luke 12:33 (Q1LK72).
185. Luke 12:34 (Q1LK73).
186. Luke 13:24 (Q1LK74).
187. Luke 14:11 (Q1LK75).
188. Luke 14:16 (Q1LK76).
189. Luke 14:17 (Q1LK77).
190. Luke 14:18 (Q1LK78).
191. Luke 14:19 (Q1LK79).
192. Luke 14:20 (Q1LK80).
193. Luke 14:21 (Q1LK81).
194. Luke 14:22 (Q1LK82).
195. Luke 14:23 (Q1LK83).
196. Luke 14:24 (Q1LK84).
197. Luke 14:26 (Q1LK85).
198. Luke 14:27 (Q1LK86).
199. Luke 14:34 (Q1LK87).
200. Luke 14:35 (Q1LK88).
201. Luke 17:1 (Q1LK89).
202. Luke 17:2 (Q1LK90).
203. Luke 17:3b (Q1LK91).
204. Luke 17:4 (Q1LK92).
205. Luke 17:5 (Q1LK93).
206. Luke 17:6 (Q1LK94).
207. Luke 17:33 (Q1LK95).
208. Luke 18:14 (Q1LK96). (END OF Q¹ IN LUKE.)
209. Sources for Q2LK: Lochlainn Seabrook; Harnack, TSOJ, pp. 127-146; Streeter, TFG, pp. 271-292; Kloppenborg, TFOQ, pp. 368-370; Kloppenborg, QP, pp. 188-189; Kloppenborg, "Redactional Strata and Social History in the Sayings Gospel Q"; Kümmel, ITTNT, pp. 65-66.
210. Luke 3:7 (Q2LK1). (BEGINNING OF Q² IN LUKE.)
211. Luke 3:8 (Q2LK2).

212. Luke 3:9 (Q2LK3).
213. Luke 3:16 (Q2LK4).
214. Luke 3:17 (Q2LK5).
215. Luke 7:1 (Q2LK6).
216. Luke 7:2 (Q2LK7).
217. Luke 7:3 (Q2LK8).
218. Luke 7:4 (Q2LK9).
219. Luke 7:5 (Q2LK10).
220. Luke 7:6 (Q2LK11).
221. Luke 7:7 (Q2LK12).
222. Luke 7:8 (Q2LK13).
223. Luke 7:9 (Q2LK14).
224. Luke 7:10 (Q2LK15).
225. Luke 7:18 (Q2LK16).
226. Luke 7:19 (Q2LK17).
227. Luke 7:20 (Q2LK18).
228. Luke 7:21 (Q2LK19).
229. Luke 7:22 (Q2LK20).
230. Luke 7:23 (Q2LK21).
231. Luke 7:24 (Q2LK22).
232. Luke 7:25 (Q2LK23).
233. Luke 7:26 (Q2LK24).
234. Luke 7:27 (Q2LK25).
235. Luke 7:28 (Q2LK26).
236. Luke 7:31 (Q2LK27).
237. Luke 7:32 (Q2LK28).
238. Luke 7:33 (Q2LK29).
239. Luke 7:34 (Q2LK30).
240. Luke 7:35 (Q2LK31).
241. Luke 11:14 (Q2LK32).
242. Luke 11:15 (Q2LK33).
243. Luke 11:16 (Q2LK34).
244. Luke 11:17 (Q2LK35).
245. Luke 11:18 (Q2LK36).
246. Luke 11:19 (Q2LK37).
247. Luke 11:20 (Q2LK38).
248. Luke 11:21 (Q2LK39).
249. Luke 11:22 (Q2LK40).
250. Luke 11:23 (Q2LK41).
251. Luke 11:24 (Q2LK42).
252. Luke 11:25 (Q2LK43).
253. Luke 11:26 (Q2LK44).
254. Luke 11:27 (Q2LK45).
255. Luke 11:28 (Q2LK46).
256. Luke 11:29 (Q2LK47).
257. Luke 11:30 (Q2LK48).
258. Luke 11:31 (Q2LK49).
259. Luke 11:32 (Q2LK50).
260. Luke 11:33 (Q2LK51).
261. Luke 11:34 (Q2LK52).
262. Luke 11:35 (Q2LK53).
263. Luke 11:36 (Q2LK54).
264. Luke 11:39b (Q2LK55).
265. Luke 11:40 (Q2LK56).
266. Luke 11:41 (Q2LK57).
267. Luke 11:42b (Q2LK58).
268. Luke 11:43 (Q2LK59).

269. Luke 11:44 (Q2LK60).
270. Luke 11:46 (Q2LK61).
271. Luke 11:47 (Q2LK62).
272. Luke 11:48 (Q2LK63).
273. Luke 11:49 (Q2LK64).
274. Luke 11:50 (Q2LK65).
275. Luke 11:51 (Q2LK66).
276. Luke 11:52 (Q2LK67).
277. Luke 12:39 (Q2LK68).
278. Luke 12:40 (Q2LK69).
279. Luke 12:42 (Q2LK70).
280. Luke 12:43 (Q2LK71).
281. Luke 12:44 (Q2LK72).
282. Luke 12:45 (Q2LK73).
283. Luke 12:46 (Q2LK74).
284. Luke 12:49 (Q2LK75).
285. Luke 12:51 (Q2LK76).
286. Luke 12:52 (Q2LK77).
287. Luke 12:53 (Q2LK78).
288. Luke 12:54 (Q2LK79).
289. Luke 12:55 (Q2LK80).
290. Luke 12:56 (Q2LK81).
291. Luke 12:57 (Q2LK82).
292. Luke 12:58 (Q2LK83).
293. Luke 12:59 (Q2LK84).
294. Luke 13:18 (Q2LK85).
295. Luke 13:19 (Q2LK86).
296. Luke 13:20 (Q2LK87).
297. Luke 13:21 (Q2LK88).
298. Luke 13:24 (Q2LK89).
299. Luke 13:25 (Q2LK90).
300. Luke 13:26 (Q2LK91).
301. Luke 13:27 (Q2LK92).
302. Luke 13:28 (Q2LK93).
303. Luke 13:29 (Q2LK94).
304. Luke 13:30 (Q2LK95).
305. Luke 13:34 (Q2LK96).
306. Luke 13:35 (Q2LK97).
307. Luke 16:16 (Q2LK98).
308. Luke 17:20 (Q2LK99).
309. Luke 17:21 (Q2LK100).
310. Luke 17:23 (Q2LK101).
311. Luke 17:24 (Q2LK102).
312. Luke 17:26 (Q2LK103).
313. Luke 17:27 (Q2LK104).
314. Luke 17:28 (Q2LK105).
315. Luke 17:29 (Q2LK106).
316. Luke 17:30 (Q2LK107).
317. Luke 17:34 (Q2LK108).
318. Luke 17:35 (Q2LK109).
319. Luke 19:12 (Q2LK110).
320. Luke 19:13 (Q2LK111).
321. Luke 19:14 (Q2LK112).
322. Luke 19:15 (Q2LK113).
323. Luke 19:16 (Q2LK114).
324. Luke 19:17 (Q2LK115).
325. Luke 19:18 (Q2LK116).

326. Luke 19:19 (Q2LK117).

327. Luke 19:20 (Q2LK118).

328. Luke 19:21 (Q2LK119).

329. Luke 19:22 (Q2LK120).

330. Luke 19:23 (Q2LK121).

331. Luke 19:24 (Q2LK122).

332. Luke 19:25 (Q2LK123).

333. Luke 19:26 (Q2LK124).

334. Luke 19:27 (Q2LK125). (END OF Q^2 IN LUKE.)

335. Sources for Q3LK: Lochlainn Seabrook; Kloppenborg, TFOQ, pp. 368-370; Kloppenborg, "Redactional Strata and Social History in the Sayings Gospel Q"; Mack, pp. 81-102.

336. Luke 4:1 (Q3LK1). (BEGINNING OF Q^3 IN LUKE.)

337. Luke 4:2 (Q3LK2).

338. Luke 4:3 (Q3LK3).

339. Luke 4:4 (Q3LK4).

340. Luke 4:5 (Q3LK5).

341. Luke 4:6 (Q3LK6).

342. Luke 4:7 (Q3LK7).

343. Luke 4:8 (Q3LK8).

344. Luke 4:9 (Q3LK9).

345. Luke 4:10 (Q3LK10).

346. Luke 4:11 (Q3LK11).

347. Luke 4:12 (Q3LK12).

348. Luke 4:13 (Q3LK13).

349. Luke 10:21 (Q3LK14).

350. Luke 10:22 (Q3LK15).

351. Luke 11:42c (Q3LK16).

352. Luke 16:17 (Q3LK17).

353. Luke 16:18 (Q3LK18).

354. Luke 22:28 (Q3LK19).

355. Luke 22:29 (Q3LK20).

356. Luke 22:30 (Q3LK21). (END OF Q^3 IN LUKE.)

357. Sources for QCLK: Lochlainn Seabrook; Harnack, TSOJ, pp. 127-146; Streeter, TFG, pp. 271-292; Kloppenborg, TFOQ, pp. 368-370; Kloppenborg, "Redactional Strata and Social History in the Sayings Gospel Q"; Kümmel, ITTNT, pp. 65-66.

358. My hypothetical reconstruction of QCLK's missing incipit (QCLK1). As such, though it is counted as a passage here in QCLK, it does not appear in and is not counted as part of either Q^1, Q^2, or Q^3. (BEGINNING OF COMPLETE Q IN LUKE.)

359. Luke 3:7 (QCLK2).

360. Luke 3:8 (QCLK3).

361. Luke 3:9 (QCLK4).

362. Luke 3:16 (QCLK5).

363. Luke 3:17 (QCLK6).

364. Luke 4:1 (QCLK7).

365. Luke 4:2 (QCLK8).

366. Luke 4:3 (QCLK9).

367. Luke 4:4 (QCLK10).

368. Luke 4:5 (QCLK11).

369. Luke 4:6 (QCLK12).

370. Luke 4:7 (QCLK13).

371. Luke 4:8 (QCLK14).

372. Luke 4:9 (QCLK15).

373. Luke 4:10 (QCLK16).

374. Luke 4:11 (QCLK17).

375. Luke 4:12 (QCLK18).

376. Luke 4:13 (QCLK19).

377. Luke 6:20b (QCLK20).

378. Luke 6:21 (QCLK21).
379. Luke 6:22 (QCLK22).
380. Luke 6:23b (QCLK23).
381. Luke 6:27 (QCLK24).
382. Luke 6:28 (QCLK25).
383. Luke 6:29 (QCLK26).
384. Luke 6:30 (QCLK27).
385. Luke 6:31 (QCLK28).
386. Luke 6:32 (QCLK29).
387. Luke 6:33 (QCLK30).
388. Luke 6:34 (QCLK31).
389. Luke 6:35 (QCLK32).
390. Luke 6:36 (QCLK33).
391. Luke 6:37 (QCLK34).
392. Luke 6:38 (QCLK35).
393. Luke 6:39 (QCLK36).
394. Luke 6:40 (QCLK37).
395. Luke 6:41 (QCLK38).
396. Luke 6:42 (QCLK39).
397. Luke 6:43 (QCLK40).
398. Luke 6:44 (QCLK41).
399. Luke 6:45 (QCLK42).
400. Luke 6:46 (QCLK43).
401. Luke 6:47 (QCLK44).
402. Luke 6:48 (QCLK45).
403. Luke 6:49 (QCLK46).
404. Luke 7:1 (QCLK47).
405. Luke 7:2 (QCLK48).
406. Luke 7:3 (QCLK49).
407. Luke 7:4 (QCLK50).
408. Luke 7:5 (QCLK51).
409. Luke 7:6 (QCLK52).
410. Luke 7:7 (QCLK53).
411. Luke 7:8 (QCLK54).
412. Luke 7:9 (QCLK55).
413. Luke 7:10 (QCLK56).
414. Luke 7:18 (QCLK57).
415. Luke 7:19 (QCLK58).
416. Luke 7:20 (QCLK59).
417. Luke 7:21 (QCLK60).
418. Luke 7:22 (QCLK61).
419. Luke 7:23 (QCLK62).
420. Luke 7:24 (QCLK63).
421. Luke 7:25 (QCLK64).
422. Luke 7:26 (QCLK65).
423. Luke 7:27 (QCLK66).
424. Luke 7:28 (QCLK67).
425. Luke 7:31 (QCLK68).
426. Luke 7:32 (QCLK69).
427. Luke 7:33 (QCLK70).
428. Luke 7:34 (QCLK71).
429. Luke 7:35 (QCLK72).
430. Luke 9:57 (QCLK73).
431. Luke 9:58 (QCLK74).
432. Luke 9:59 (QCLK75).
433. Luke 9:60 (QCLK76).
434. Luke 9:61 (QCLK77).

435. Luke 9:62 (QCLK78).
436. Luke 10:2 (QCLK79).
437. Luke 10:3 (QCLK80).
438. Luke 10:4 (QCLK81).
439. Luke 10:5 (QCLK82).
440. Luke 10:6 (QCLK83).
441. Luke 10:7 (QCLK84).
442. Luke 10:8 (QCLK85).
443. Luke 10:9 (QCLK86).
444. Luke 10:10 (QCLK87).
445. Luke 10:11 (QCLK88).
446. Luke 10:16 (QCLK89).
447. Luke 10:21 (QCLK90).
448. Luke 10:22 (QCLK91).
449. Luke 11:2 (QCLK92).
450. Luke 11:3 (QCLK93).
451. Luke 11:4 (QCLK94).
452. Luke 11:9 (QCLK95).
453. Luke 11:10 (QCLK96).
454. Luke 11:11 (QCLK97).
455. Luke 11:12 (QCLK98).
456. Luke 11:13 (QCLK99).
457. Luke 11:14 (QCLK100).
458. Luke 11:15 (QCLK101).
459. Luke 11:16 (QCLK102).
460. Luke 11:17 (QCLK103).
461. Luke 11:18 (QCLK104).
462. Luke 11:19 (QCLK105).
463. Luke 11:20 (QCLK106).
464. Luke 11:21 (QCLK107).
465. Luke 11:22 (QCLK108).
466. Luke 11:23 (QCLK109).
467. Luke 11:24 (QCLK110).
468. Luke 11:25 (QCLK111).
469. Luke 11:26 (QCLK112).
470. Luke 11:27 (QCLK113).
471. Luke 11:28 (QCLK114).
472. Luke 11:29 (QCLK115).
473. Luke 11:30 (QCLK116).
474. Luke 11:31 (QCLK117).
475. Luke 11:32 (QCLK118).
476. Luke 11:33 (QCLK119).
477. Luke 11:34 (QCLK120).
478. Luke 11:35 (QCLK121).
479. Luke 11:36 (QCLK122).
480. Luke 11:39b (QCLK123).
481. Luke 11:40 (QCLK124).
482. Luke 11:41 (QCLK125).
483. Luke 11:42b,c (QCLK126).
484. Luke 11:43 (QCLK127).
485. Luke 11:44 (QCLK128).
486. Luke 11:46 (QCLK129).
487. Luke 11:47 (QCLK130).
488. Luke 11:48 (QCLK131).
489. Luke 11:49 (QCLK132).
490. Luke 11:50 (QCLK133).
491. Luke 11:51 (QCLK134).

492. Luke 11:52 (QCLK135).
493. Luke 12:2 (QCLK136).
494. Luke 12:3 (QCLK137).
495. Luke 12:4 (QCLK138).
496. Luke 12:5 (QCLK139).
497. Luke 12:6 (QCLK140).
498. Luke 12:7 (QCLK141).
499. Luke 12:11 (QCLK142).
500. Luke 12:12 (QCLK143).
501. Luke 12:22b (QCLK144).
502. Luke 12:23 (QCLK145).
503. Luke 12:24 (QCLK146).
504. Luke 12:25 (QCLK147).
505. Luke 12:26 (QCLK148).
506. Luke 12:27 (QCLK149).
507. Luke 12:28 (QCLK150).
508. Luke 12:29 (QCLK151).
509. Luke 12:30 (QCLK152).
510. Luke 12:31 (QCLK153).
511. Luke 12:33 (QCLK154).
512. Luke 12:34 (QCLK155).
513. Luke 12:39 (QCLK156).
514. Luke 12:40 (QCLK157).
515. Luke 12:42 (QCLK158).
516. Luke 12:43 (QCLK159).
517. Luke 12:44 (QCLK160).
518. Luke 12:45 (QCLK161).
519. Luke 12:46 (QCLK162).
520. Luke 12:49 (QCLK163).
521. Luke 12:51 (QCLK164).
522. Luke 12:52 (QCLK165).
523. Luke 12:53 (QCLK166).
524. Luke 12:54 (QCLK167).
525. Luke 12:55 (QCLK168).
526. Luke 12:56 (QCLK169).
527. Luke 12:57 (QCLK170).
528. Luke 12:58 (QCLK171).
529. Luke 12:59 (QCLK172).
530. Luke 13:18 (QCLK173).
531. Luke 13:19 (QCLK174).
532. Luke 13:20 (QCLK175).
533. Luke 13:21 (QCLK176).
534. Luke 13:24 (QCLK177).
535. Luke 13:25 (QCLK178).
536. Luke 13:26 (QCLK179).
537. Luke 13:27 (QCLK180).
538. Luke 13:28 (QCLK181).
539. Luke 13:29 (QCLK182).
540. Luke 13:30 (QCLK183).
541. Luke 13:34 (QCLK184).
542. Luke 13:35 (QCLK185).
543. Luke 14:11 (QCLK186).
544. Luke 14:16 (QCLK187).
545. Luke 14:17 (QCLK188).
546. Luke 14:18 (QCLK189).
547. Luke 14:19 (QCLK190).
548. Luke 14:20 (QCLK191).

549. Luke 14:21 (QCLK192).
550. Luke 14:22 (QCLK193).
551. Luke 14:23 (QCLK194).
552. Luke 14:24 (QCLK195).
553. Luke 14:26 (QCLK196).
554. Luke 14:27 (QCLK197).
555. Luke 14:34 (QCLK198).
556. Luke 14:35 (QCLK199).
557. Luke 16:16 (QCLK200).
558. Luke 16:17 (QCLK201).
559. Luke 16:18 (QCLK202).
560. Luke 17:1 (QCLK203).
561. Luke 17:2 (QCLK204).
562. Luke 17:3b (QCLK205).
563. Luke 17:4 (QCLK206).
564. Luke 17:5 (QCLK207).
565. Luke 17:6 (QCLK208).
566. Luke 17:20 (QCLK209).
567. Luke 17:21 (QCLK210).
568. Luke 17:23 (QCLK211).
569. Luke 17:24 (QCLK212).
570. Luke 17:26 (QCLK213).
571. Luke 17:27 (QCLK214).
572. Luke 17:28 (QCLK215).
573. Luke 17:29 (QCLK216).
574. Luke 17:30 (QCLK217).
575. Luke 17:33 (QCLK218).
576. Luke 17:34 (QCLK219).
577. Luke 17:35 (QCLK220).
578. Luke 18:14 (QCLK221).
579. Luke 19:12 (QCLK222).
580. Luke 19:13 (QCLK223).
581. Luke 19:14 (QCLK224).
582. Luke 19:15 (QCLK225).
583. Luke 19:16 (QCLK226).
584. Luke 19:17 (QCLK227).
585. Luke 19:18 (QCLK228).
586. Luke 19:19 (QCLK229).
587. Luke 19:20 (QCLK230).
588. Luke 19:21 (QCLK231).
589. Luke 19:22 (QCLK232).
590. Luke 19:23 (QCLK233).
591. Luke 19:24 (QCLK234).
592. Luke 19:25 (QCLK235).
593. Luke 19:26 (QCLK236).
594. Luke 19:27 (QCLK237).
595. Luke 22:28 (QCLK238).
596. Luke 22:29 (QCLK239).
597. Luke 22:30 (QCLK240). (END OF COMPLETE Q IN LUKE.)
598. Source for QCMK: Lochlainn Seabrook.
599. My hypothetical reconstruction of QCMK's missing incipit (QCMK1). (BEGINNING OF COMPLETE Q IN MARK.)
600. Mark 1:2 (QCMK2).
601. Mark 1:7 (QCMK3).
602. Mark 1:8 (QCMK4).
603. Mark 1:12 (QCMK5).
604. Mark 1:13 (QCMK6).

605. Mark 3:22 (QCMK7).
606. Mark 3:23 (QCMK8).
607. Mark 3:24 (QCMK9).
608. Mark 3:25 (QCMK10).
609. Mark 3:26 (QCMK11).
610. Mark 3:27 (QCMK12).
611. Mark 4:21 (QCMK13).
612. Mark 4:22 (QCMK14).
613. Mark 4:24 (QCMK15).
614. Mark 4:30 (QCMK16).
615. Mark 4:31 (QCMK17).
616. Mark 4:32 (QCMK18).
617. Mark 6:7 (QCMK19).
618. Mark 6:8 (QCMK20).
619. Mark 6:9 (QCMK21).
620. Mark 6:10 (QCMK22).
621. Mark 6:11 (QCMK23).
622. Mark 8:34 (QCMK24).
623. Mark 8:38 (QCMK25).
624. Mark 9:49 (QCMK26).
625. Mark 9:50 (QCMK27).
626. Mark 12:38 (QCMK28).
627. Mark 12:39 (QCMK29).
628. Mark 12:40 (QCMK30).
629. Mark 13:11 (QCMK31).
630. Mark 13:21 (QCMK32).
631. Mark 13:33 (QCMK33).
632. Mark 13:34 (QCMK34).
633. Mark 13:35 (QCMK35).
634. Mark 13:36 (QCMK36). (END OF COMPLETE Q IN MARK.)
635. Source for C1MT: Lochlainn Seabrook.
636. My hypothetical reconstruction of Q1MT's missing incipit (Q1MT1). (BEGINNING OF Q¹ IN MATTHEW.)
637. Matthew 5:3 (Q1MT2).
638. Matthew 5:4 (Q1MT3).
639. Matthew 5:6 (Q1MT4).
640. Matthew 5:11 (Q1MT5).
641. Matthew 5:12 (Q1MT6).
642. Matthew 5:13 (Q1MT7).
643. Matthew 5:39 (Q1MT8).
644. Matthew 5:40 (Q1MT9).
645. Matthew 5:42 (Q1MT10).
646. Matthew 5:44 (Q1MT11).
647. Matthew 5:46 (Q1MT12).
648. Matthew 5:47 (Q1MT13).
649. Matthew 5:48 (Q1MT14).
650. Matthew 6:9 (Q1MT15).
651. Matthew 6:10 (Q1MT16).
652. Matthew 6:11 (Q1MT17).
653. Matthew 6:12 (Q1MT18).
654. Matthew 6:13 (Q1MT19).
655. Matthew 6:19 (Q1MT20).
656. Matthew 6:20 (Q1MT21).
657. Matthew 6:21 (Q1MT22).
658. Matthew 6:25 (Q1MT23).
659. Matthew 6:26 (Q1MT24).
660. Matthew 6:27 (Q1MT25).
661. Matthew 6:28 (Q1MT26).

662. Matthew 6:29 (Q1MT27).
663. Matthew 6:30 (Q1MT28).
664. Matthew 6:31 (Q1MT29).
665. Matthew 6:32 (Q1MT30).
666. Matthew 6:33 (Q1MT31).
667. Matthew 7:1 (Q1MT32).
668. Matthew 7:2 (Q1MT33).
669. Matthew 7:3 (Q1MT34).
670. Matthew 7:4 (Q1MT35).
671. Matthew 7:5 (Q1MT36).
672. Matthew 7:7 (Q1MT37).
673. Matthew 7:8 (Q1MT38).
674. Matthew 7:9 (Q1MT39).
675. Matthew 7:11 (Q1MT40).
676. Matthew 7:12 (Q1MT41).
677. Matthew 7:16 (Q1MT42).
678. Matthew 7:18 (Q1MT43).
679. Matthew 7:21 (Q1MT44).
680. Matthew 7:24 (Q1MT45).
681. Matthew 7:25 (Q1MT46).
682. Matthew 7:26 (Q1MT47).
683. Matthew 7:27 (Q1MT48).
684. Matthew 8:19 (Q1MT49).
685. Matthew 8:20 (Q1MT50).
686. Matthew 8:21 (Q1MT51).
687. Matthew 8:22 (Q1MT52).
688. Matthew 9:37 (Q1MT53).
689. Matthew 9:38 (Q1MT54).
690. Matthew 10:7 (Q1MT55).
691. Matthew 10:8 (Q1MT56).
692. Matthew 10:9 (Q1MT57).
693. Matthew 10:10 (Q1MT58).
694. Matthew 10:12 (Q1MT59).
695. Matthew 10:13 (Q1MT60).
696. Matthew 10:14 (Q1MT61).
697. Matthew 10:16 (Q1MT62).
698. Matthew 10:24 (Q1MT63).
699. Matthew 10:26 (Q1MT64).
700. Matthew 10:27 (Q1MT65).
701. Matthew 10:28 (Q1MT66).
702. Matthew 10:29 (Q1MT67).
703. Matthew 10:30 (Q1MT68).
704. Matthew 10:31 (Q1MT69).
705. Matthew 10:37 (Q1MT70).
706. Matthew 10:38 (Q1MT71).
707. Matthew 12:34 (Q1MT72).
708. Matthew 12:35 (Q1MT73).
709. Matthew 13:31 (Q1MT74).
710. Matthew 13:32 (Q1MT75).
711. Matthew 13:33 (Q1MT76).
712. Matthew 15:14 (Q1MT77).
713. Matthew 22:1 (Q1MT78).
714. Matthew 22:2 (Q1MT79)
715. Matthew 22:3 (Q1MT80).
716. Matthew 22:4 (Q1MT81).
717. Matthew 22:5 (Q1MT82).
718. Matthew 22:6 (Q1MT83).

719. Matthew 22:7 (Q1MT84).
720. Matthew 22:8 (Q1MT85).
721. Matthew 22:9 (Q1MT86).
722. Matthew 22:10 (Q1MT87).
723. Matthew 23:12 (Q1MT88). (END OF Q¹ IN MATTHEW.)
724. Sources for QCMT: Lochlainn Seabrook; Kümmel, ITTNT, pp. 65-66.
725. My hypothetical reconstruction of QCMT's missing incipit (QCMT1). (BEGINNING OF COMPLETE Q IN MATTHEW.)
726. Matthew 3:7 (QCMT2).
727. Matthew 3:8 (QCMT3).
728. Matthew 3:9 (QCMT4).
729. Matthew 3:10 (QCMT5).
730. Matthew 3:11 (QCMT6).
731. Matthew 3:12 (QCMT7).
732. Matthew 4:1 (QCMT8).
733. Matthew 4:2 (QCMT9).
734. Matthew 4:3 (QCMT10).
735. Matthew 4:4 (QCMT11).
736. Matthew 4:5 (QCMT12).
737. Matthew 4:6 (QCMT13).
738. Matthew 4:7 (QCMT14).
739. Matthew 4:8 (QCMT15).
740. Matthew 4:9 (QCMT16).
741. Matthew 4:10 (QCMT17).
742. Matthew 4:11 (QCMT18).
743. Matthew 5:3 (QCMT19).
744. Matthew 5:4 (QCMT20).
745. Matthew 5:6 (QCMT21).
746. Matthew 5:11 (QCMT22).
747. Matthew 5:12 (QCMT23).
748. Matthew 5:13 (QCMT24).
749. Matthew 5:15 (QCMT25).
750. Matthew 5:18 (QCMT26).
751. Matthew 5:25 (QCMT27).
752. Matthew 5:26 (QCMT28).
753. Matthew 5:32 (QCMT29).
754. Matthew 5:39 (QCMT30).
755. Matthew 5:40 (QCMT31).
756. Matthew 5:42 (QCMT32).
757. Matthew 5:44 (QCMT33).
758. Matthew 5:45 (QCMT34).
759. Matthew 5:46 (QCMT35).
760. Matthew 5:47 (QCMT36).
761. Matthew 5:48 (QCMT37).
762. Matthew 6:9 (QCMT38).
763. Matthew 6:10 (QCMT39).
764. Matthew 6:11 (QCMT40).
765. Matthew 6:12 (QCMT41).
766. Matthew 6:13 (QCMT42).
767. Matthew 6:19 (QCMT43).
768. Matthew 6:20 (QCMT44).
769. Matthew 6:21 (QCMT45).
770. Matthew 6:22 (QCMT46).
771. Matthew 6:23 (QCMT47).
772. Matthew 6:24 (QCMT48).
773. Matthew 6:25 (QCMT49).
774. Matthew 6:26 (QCMT50).

775. Matthew 6:27 (QCMT51).
776. Matthew 6:28 (QCMT52).
777. Matthew 6:29 (QCMT53).
778. Matthew 6:30 (QCMT54).
779. Matthew 6:31 (QCMT55).
780. Matthew 6:32 (QCMT56).
781. Matthew 6:33 (QCMT57).
782. Matthew 7:1 (QCMT58).
783. Matthew 7:2 (QCMT59).
784. Matthew 7:3 (QCMT60).
785. Matthew 7:4 (QCMT61).
786. Matthew 7:5 (QCMT62).
787. Matthew 7:7 (QCMT63).
788. Matthew 7:8 (QCMT64).
789. Matthew 7:9 (QCMT65).
790. Matthew 7:10 (QCMT66).
791. Matthew 7:11 (QCMT67).
792. Matthew 7:12 (QCMT68).
793. Matthew 7:13 (QCMT69).
794. Matthew 7:14 (QCMT70).
795. Matthew 7:16 (QCMT71).
796. Matthew 7:17 (QCMT72).
797. Matthew 7:18 (QCMT73).
798. Matthew 7:21 (QCMT74).
799. Matthew 7:22 (QCMT75).
800. Matthew 7:23 (QCMT76).
801. Matthew 7:24 (QCMT77).
802. Matthew 7:25 (QCMT78).
803. Matthew 7:26 (QCMT79).
804. Matthew 7:27 (QCMT80).
805. Matthew 8:5 (QCMT81).
806. Matthew 8:6 (QCMT82).
807. Matthew 8:7 (QCMT83).
808. Matthew 8:8 (QCMT84).
809. Matthew 8:9 (QCMT85).
810. Matthew 8:10 (QCMT86).
811. Matthew 8:11 (QCMT87).
812. Matthew 8:12 (QCMT88).
813. Matthew 8:13 (QCMT89).
814. Matthew 8:19 (QCMT90).
815. Matthew 8:20 (QCMT91).
816. Matthew 8:21 (QCMT92).
817. Matthew 8:22 (QCMT93).
818. Matthew 9:37 (QCMT94).
819. Matthew 9:38 (QCMT95).
820. Matthew 10:7 (QCMT96).
821. Matthew 10:8 (QCMT97).
822. Matthew 10:9 (QCMT98).
823. Matthew 10:10 (QCMT99).
824. Matthew 10:11 (QCMT100).
825. Matthew 10:12 (QCMT101).
826. Matthew 10:13 (QCMT102).
827. Matthew 10:14 (QCMT103).
828. Matthew 10:15 (QCMT104).
829. Matthew 10:16 (QCMT105).
830. Matthew 10:24 (QCMT106).
831. Matthew 10:25 (QCMT107).

832. Matthew 10:26 (QCMT108).
833. Matthew 10:27 (QCMT109).
834. Matthew 10:28 (QCMT110).
835. Matthew 10:29 (QCMT111).
836. Matthew 10:30 (QCMT112).
837. Matthew 10:31 (QCMT113).
838. Matthew 10:32 (QCMT114).
839. Matthew 10:33 (QCMT115).
840. Matthew 10:34 (QCMT116).
841. Matthew 10:35 (QCMT117).
842. Matthew 10:36 (QCMT118).
843. Matthew 10:37 (QCMT119).
844. Matthew 10:38 (QCMT120).
845. Matthew 10:39 (QCMT121).
846. Matthew 10:40 (QCMT122).
847. Matthew 11:2 (QCMT123).
848. Matthew 11:3 (QCMT124).
849. Matthew 11:4 (QCMT125).
850. Matthew 11:5 (QCMT126).
851. Matthew 11:6 (QCMT127).
852. Matthew 11:7 (QCMT128).
853. Matthew 11:8 (QCMT129).
854. Matthew 11:9 (QCMT130).
855. Matthew 11:10 (QCMT131).
856. Matthew 11:11 (QCMT132).
857. Matthew 11:12 (QCMT133).
858. Matthew 11:13 (QCMT134).
859. Matthew 11:16 (QCMT135).
860. Matthew 11:17 (QCMT136).
861. Matthew 11:18 (QCMT137).
862. Matthew 11:19 (QCMT138).
863. Matthew 11:20 (QCMT139).
864. Matthew 11:21 (QCMT140).
865. Matthew 11:22 (QCMT141).
866. Matthew 11:23 (QCMT142).
867. Matthew 11:24 (QCMT143).
868. Matthew 11:25 (QCMT144).
869. Matthew 11:26 (QCMT145).
870. Matthew 11:27 (QCMT146).
871. Matthew 12:22 (QCMT147).
872. Matthew 12:23 (QCMT148).
873. Matthew 12:24 (QCMT149).
874. Matthew 12:25 (QCMT150).
875. Matthew 12:26 (QCMT151).
876. Matthew 12:27 (QCMT152).
877. Matthew 12:28 (QCMT153).
878. Matthew 12:29 (QCMT154).
879. Matthew 12:30 (QCMT155).
880. Matthew 12:32 (QCMT156).
881. Matthew 12:33 (QCMT157).
882. Matthew 12:38 (QCMT158).
883. Matthew 12:39 (QCMT159).
884. Matthew 12:40 (QCMT160).
885. Matthew 12:41 (QCMT161).
886. Matthew 12:42 (QCMT162).
887. Matthew 12:43 (QCMT163).
888. Matthew 12:44 (QCMT164).

889. Matthew 12:45 (QCMT165).
890. Matthew 13:16 (QCMT166).
891. Matthew 13:17 (QCMT167).
892. Matthew 13:31 (QCMT168).
893. Matthew 13:32 (QCMT169).
894. Matthew 13:33 (QCMT170).
895. Matthew 15:14 (QCMT171).
896. Matthew 16:2 (QCMT172).
897. Matthew 16:3 (QCMT173).
898. Matthew 17:20 (QCMT174).
899. Matthew 18:6 (QCMT175).
900. Matthew 18:7 (QCMT176).
901. Matthew 18:12 (QCMT177).
902. Matthew 18:13 (QCMT178).
903. Matthew 18:14 (QCMT179).
904. Matthew 18:15 (QCMT180).
905. Matthew 18:21 (QCMT181).
906. Matthew 18:22 (QCMT182).
907. Matthew 19:28 (QCMT183).
908. Matthew 21:31 (QCMT184).
909. Matthew 21:32 (QCMT185).
910. Matthew 22:2 (QCMT186).
911. Matthew 22:3 (QCMT187).
912. Matthew 22:4 (QCMT188).
913. Matthew 22:5 (QCMT189).
914. Matthew 22:6 (QCMT190).
915. Matthew 22:7 (QCMT191).
916. Matthew 22:8 (QCMT192).
917. Matthew 22:9 (QCMT193).
918. Matthew 22:10 (QCMT194).
919. Matthew 23:4 (QCMT195).
920. Matthew 23:6 (QCMT196).
921. Matthew 23:7a (QCMT197).
922. Matthew 23:12 (QCMT198).
923. Matthew 23:13 (QCMT199).
924. Matthew 23:23 (QCMT200).
925. Matthew 23:25 (QCMT201).
926. Matthew 23:26 (QCMT202).
927. Matthew 23:27 (QCMT203).
928. Matthew 23:29 (QCMT204).
929. Matthew 23:30 (QCMT205).
930. Matthew 23:31 (QCMT206).
931. Matthew 23:34 (QCMT207).
932. Matthew 23:35 (QCMT208).
933. Matthew 23:36 (QCMT209).
934. Matthew 23:37 (QCMT210).
935. Matthew 23:38 (QCMT211).
936. Matthew 23:39 (QCMT212).
937. Matthew 24:26 (QCMT213).
938. Matthew 24:27 (QCMT214).
939. Matthew 24:28 (QCMT215).
940. Matthew 24:37 (QCMT216).
941. Matthew 24:38 (QCMT217).
942. Matthew 24:39 (QCMT218).
943. Matthew 24:40 (QCMT219).
944. Matthew 24:41 (QCMT220).
945. Matthew 24:43 (QCMT221).

946. Matthew 24:44 (QCMT222).
947. Matthew 24:45 (QCMT223).
948. Matthew 24:46 (QCMT224).
949. Matthew 24:47 (QCMT225).
950. Matthew 24:48 (QCMT226).
951. Matthew 24:49 (QCMT227).
952. Matthew 24:50 (QCMT228).
953. Matthew 24:51 (QCMT229).
954. Matthew 25:14 (QCMT230).
955. Matthew 25:15 (QCMT231).
956. Matthew 25:16 (QCMT232).
957. Matthew 25:17 (QCMT233).
958. Matthew 25:18 (QCMT234).
959. Matthew 25:19 (QCMT235).
960. Matthew 25:20 (QCMT236).
961. Matthew 25:21 (QCMT237).
962. Matthew 25:22 (QCMT238).
963. Matthew 25:23 (QCMT239).
964. Matthew 25:24 (QCMT240).
965. Matthew 25:25 (QCMT241).
966. Matthew 25:26 (QCMT242).
967. Matthew 25:27 (QCMT243).
968. Matthew 25:28 (QCMT244).
969. Matthew 25:29 (QCMT245).
970. Matthew 25:30 (QCMT246). (END OF COMPLETE Q IN MATTHEW.)

BIBLIOGRAPHY
And Suggested Reading

Angus, Samuel. *The Mystery-Religions and Christianity: A Study of the Religious Background of Early Christianity*. 1925. New York, NY: Citadel Press, 1966 ed.

Bewer, Julius A. *The Literature of the Old Testament in Its Historical Development*. New York, NY: Columbia University Press, 1922.

Barnstone, Willis (ed.). *The Other Bible*. San Francisco, CA: Harper and Row, 1984.

Boardman, John, Jasper Griffin, and Oswyn Murray. *The Roman World*. 1986. Oxford, UK: Oxford University Press, 1988 ed.

Borg, Marcus (ed.). *The Lost Gospel Q: The Original Sayings of Jesus*. 1996. Berkeley, CA: Ulysses Press, 1999 ed.

Boring, Eugene M. *Sayings of the Risen Jesus: Christian Prophecy in the Synoptic Tradition*. Cambridge, UK: Cambridge University Press, 1982.

Butler, Trent C. (ed.). *Holman Bible Dictionary*. Nashville, TN: Holman, 1991.

Campbell, Joseph. *Occidental Mythology: The Masks of God*. 1964. New York, NY: Arkana, 1991 ed.

Christie-Murray, David. *A History of Heresy*. 1976. Oxford, UK: Oxford University Press, 1990 ed.

Cotterell, Arthur. *The Macmillan Illustrated Encyclopedia of Myths and Legends*. New York, NY: Macmillan, 1989.

Courtenay, William J. (ed.). *The Judeo-Christian Heritage*. New York, NY: Holt, Rinehart and Winston, 1970.

Cross, F. L., and E. A. Livingstone (eds.). *The Oxford Dictionary of the Christian Church*. 1957. London, UK: Oxford University Press, 1974 ed.

Crusé, Christian Frederick. *The Ecclesiastical History of Eusebius Pamphilus, Bishop of Cesarea, in Palestine*. New York, NY: Stanford and Swords, 1850.

Dowley, Tim (ed.). *The History of Christianity*. Oxford, UK: Lion, 1977.

Dunn, James D. G. *Jesus Remembered*. Grand Rapids, MI: William B. Eerdmans, 2003.

Edwards, Richard A. *A Theology of Q: Eschatology, Prophecy, and Wisdom*. Philadelphia, PA: Fortress Press, 1976.

Eisenman, Robert, and Michael Wise. *The Dead Sea Scrolls Uncovered*. Rockport, MA: Element, 1992.

Eisler, Robert. *The Messiah Jesus and John the Baptist: According to Flavius Josephus' Recently Rediscovered 'Capture of Jerusalem' and the Other Jewish and Christian Sources*. London, UK: Methuen, 1931.

Fillmore, Charles. *Metaphysical Bible Dictionary*. Unity Village, MO: Unity School of Christianity, 1931.

Finigan, Jack. *Light From the Ancient Past: The Archaeological Background of the Hebrew-Christian Religion* (Vol. 1). 1946. Princeton, NJ: Princeton University

Press, 1974 ed.

Frazer, James George. *The Golden Bough: A Study in Comparative Religion.* 2 vols. London, UK: Macmillan, 1890.

——. *Folk-Lore in the Old Testament: Studies in Comparative Religion, Legend, and Law.* 3 vols. London, UK: Macmillan and Co., 1919.

Gaskell, G. A. *Dictionary of All Scripture and Myths.* 1960. New York, NY: Julian Press, 1973 ed.

Gimbutas, Marija. *The Goddesses and Gods of Old Europe: 6500-3500 BC, Myths and Cult Images.* 1974. Berkeley, CA: University of California Press, 1992 ed.

Goguel, Maurice. *Jesus and the Origins of Christianity.* 2 vols. 1932. New York, NY: Harper, 1960 ed.

Goodspeed, Edgar J. *The Making of the English New Testament.* Chicago, IL: University of Chicago Press, 1925.

——. *The Formation of the New Testament.* Chicago, IL: University of Chicago Press, 1926.

——. *The Story of the Bible.* Chicago, IL: University of Chicago Press, 1936.

——. *An Introduction to the New Testament.* Chicago, IL: University of Chicago Press, 1937.

——. *The Story of the Apocrypha.* Chicago, IL: University of Chicago Press, 1939.

——. *How Came the Bible?* Nashville, TN: Abingdon Press, 1940.

——. *Christianity Goes to Press.* New York, NY: Macmillan, 1940.

Goring, Rosemary (ed.). *Larousse Dictionary of Beliefs and Religions: A Comprehensive Outline of Spiritual Concepts From Prehistory to the Present.* 1992. Edinburgh, Scotland: Larousse, 1995 ed.

Graham, Lloyd M. *Deceptions and Myths of the Bible.* 1975. New York, NY: Citadel Press, 1991 ed.

Graves, Robert. *The White Goddess: A Historical Grammar of Poetic Myth.* 1948. New York, NY: Noonday Press, 1991 ed.

——. *The Greek Myths* (combined ed.). 1955. Harmondsworth, UK: Penguin, 1992 ed.

Graves, Robert, and Raphael Patai. *Hebrew Myths: The Book of Genesis.* 1964. New York, NY: Anchor, 1989 ed.

Guignebert, Charles. *The Christ.* 1943. New York, NY: Citadel, 1968 ed.

Hall, Manly Palmer. *The Secret Teachings of All Ages: An Encyclopedic Outline of Masonic, Hermetic, Qabbalistic and Rosicrucian Symbolical Philosophy.* 1925. Los Angeles, CA: Philosophical Research Society, 1989 ed.

Harnack, Adolf. *Christianity and History.* London, UK: Adam and Charles Black, 1896.

——. *History of Dogma.* Boston, MA: Little, Brown, and Co., 1905.

——. *The Expansion of Christianity in the First Three Centuries.* (Vol. 2.) New York, NY: G. P. Putnam's Sons, 1905.

——. *The Sayings of Jesus: The Second Source of St. Matthew and St. Luke.* London, UK: Williams and Norgate, 1908.

——. *What is Christianity?* New York, NY: G. P. Putnam's Sons, 1908.

——. *The Acts of the Apostles*. New York, NY: G. P. Putnam's Sons, 1909.

——. *Bible Reading in the Early Church*. London, UK: Williams and Norgate, 1912.

Hawkins, John Caesar. *Horae Synopticae: Contributions to the Study of the Synoptic Problem*. Oxford, UK: Clarendon Press, 1899.

Hoeller, Stephan A. *Jung and the Lost Gospels: Insights Into the Dead Sea Scrolls and the Nag Hammadi Library*. Wheaton, IL: Quest Books, 1990.

Hooke, S. H. *Middle Eastern Mythology: From the Assyrians to the Hebrews*. 1963. Harmondsworth, UK: Penguin, 1991 ed.

Inge, William Ralph. *Christian Mysticism*. London, UK: Methuen and Co., 1899.

Jackson, John G. *Pagan Origins of the Christ Myth*. Austin, TX: The American Atheist Press, n.d.

Jennings, Hargrave. *The Rosicrucians: Their Rites and Mysteries*. London, UK: John Camden Hotten, 1870.

Jülicher, Adolf. *An Introduction to the New Testament*. London, UK: Smith, Elder, and Co., 1904.

Keble, John. *Five Books of S. Irenaeus: Against Heresies*. London, UK: James Parker and Co., 1872.

Kee, Howard Clark. *The Origins of Christianity: Sources and Documents*. Englewood Cliffs, NJ: Prentice-Hall, 1973.

Kelly, J. N. D. *Early Christian Doctrines*. 1960. New York, NY: Harper and Row, 1978 ed.

Kloppenborg, John S. *Q Parallels: Synopsis, Critical Notes and Concordance*. Sonoma, CA: Polebridge Press, 1988 ed.

——. "Redactional Strata and Social History in the Sayings Gospel Q," paper presented at the 124th annual meeting of the Society of Biblical Literature (Q Seminar), Chicago, IL, November 1988.

——. *Excavating Q: The History and Setting of the Sayings Gospel*. Minneapolis, MN: Fortress Press, 2000.

——. *The Formation of Q: Trajectories in Ancient Wisdom Collections*. Minneapolis, MN: Fortress Press, 2007.

——. *Q, the Earliest Gospel: An Introduction to the Original Stories and Sayings of Jesus*. Louisville, KY: Westminster John Knox Press, 2008.

Kümmel, Werner Georg. *Introduction to the New Testament*. 1973. Nashville, TN: Abingdon, 1975 ed.

Küng, Hans. *Christianity: Essence, History, and Future*. New York, NY: Continuum, 1995.

Lamsa, George M. *The Holy Bible: From Ancient Eastern Manuscripts*. 1933. Philadelphia, PA: A. J. Holman, 1968 ed.

Levi. *The Aquarian Gospel of Jesus the Christ: The Philosophic and Practical Basis of the Religion of the Aquarian Age of the World and of the Church Universal*. Los Angeles, CA: E. S. Dowling, 1911.

Lewis, H. Spencer. *The Secret Doctrines of Jesus*. 1937. San Jose, CA: The Rosicrucian Press, 1979 ed.

Lightfoot, Joseph Barber. *The Apostolic Fathers*. 2 vols. London, UK: Macmillan,

1889.

Livingstone, Elizabeth Anne (ed.). *The Concise Oxford Dictionary of the Christian Church.* 1977. Oxford, UK: Oxford University Press, 1990 ed.

Loetscher, Lefferts A. *Twentieth Century Encyclopedia of Religious Knowledge.* Grand Rapids, MI: Baker Book House, 1955.

Mack, Burton L. *The Lost Gospel: The Book of Q and Christian Origins.* San Francisco, CA: Harper Collins, 1993.

Marshall, David. *Why the Jesus Seminar Can't Find Jesus and Grandma Marshall Could: A Populist Defense of the Gospels.* Fall City, WA: Kuai Mu Press, 2005.

McKenzie, John L. *Dictionary of the Bible.* New York, NY: Collier, 1965.

Metford, J. C. J. *Dictionary of Christian Lore and Legend.* London, UK: Thames and Hudson, 1983.

Metzger, Bruce M., and Michael D. Coogan (eds.). *The Oxford Companion to the Bible.* New York, NY: Oxford University Press, 1993.

Meyer, Marvin W. (ed.). *The Ancient Mysteries: A Sourcebook.* San Francisco, CA: Harper and Row, 1987.

Miller, Robert J. (ed.). *The Complete Gospels.* 1992. Sonoma, CA: Polebridge Press, 1994 ed.

Milligan, George. *Here and There Among the Papyri.* London, UK: Hodder and Stoughton, 1922.

———. *The New Testament and Its Transmission.* London, UK: Hodder and Stoughton, 1932.

Mish, Frederick (ed.). *Webster's Ninth New Collegiate Dictionary.* 1828. Springfield, MA: Merriam-Webster, 1984 ed.

Moltmann, Jürgen. *The Crucified God: The Cross of Christ as the Foundation and Criticism of Christian Theology.* 1973. New York, NY: Harper and Row, 1974 ed.

Muller, Herbert J. *The Uses of the Past: Profiles of Former Societies.* 1952. New York, NY: Galaxy, 1963 ed.

Oesterley, W. O. E. *An Introduction to the Books of the Apocrypha.* New York, NY: Macmillan, 1935.

Orton, David E. (ed.). *The Synoptic Problem and Q: Selected Studies From Novum Testamentum.* Leiden, The Netherlands: Brill, 1999.

Pagels, Elaine. *The Gnostic Gospels.* 1979. New York, NY: Vintage, 1981 ed.

Patai, Raphael. *The Hebrew Goddess.* 1967. Detroit, MI: Wayne State University Press, 1990 ed.

Pike, Albert (ed.). *Morals and Dogmas of the Ancient and Accepted Scottish Rite of Freemasonry.* Charleston, SC: L. H. Jenkins, 1871.

Piper, Ronald A. (ed.). *The Gospel Behind the Gospels: Current Studies on Q.* Leiden, The Netherlands: E. J. Brill, 1995.

Platt, Rutherford (ed.). *The Lost Books of the Bible and the Forgotten Books of Eden.* 1927. New York, NY: Meridian, 1974 ed.

Potter, Charles Francis. *The Lost Years of Jesus Revealed.* 1958. New York, NY: Fawcett, 1962 ed.

Price, Ira M. *The Ancestry of Our English Bible.* New York, NY: Harpers, 1934.

Prophet, Mark L., and Elizabeth Clare Prophet. *The Lost Teachings of Jesus.* Livingston, MT: Summit University Press, 1986.

Richardson, Cyril C. (ed. and trans.) *Early Christian Fathers.* New York, NY: Collier, 1970.

Robertson, Archibald (trans.). *St. Athanasius on the Incarnation.* London, UK: D. Nutt, 1885.

Robertson, John M. *Christianity and Mythology.* London, UK: Watts and Co., 1900.

——. *Pagan Christs.* 1903. New York, NY: Dorset Press, 1987 ed.

Robinson, James M. (ed.). *The Nag Hammadi Library.* 1978. San Francisco, CA: Harper Collins, 1990 ed.

Robinson, James M., Paul Hoffman, and John S. Kloppenborg (eds.). *The Sayings Gospel Q in Greek and English With Parallels From the Gospels of Mark and Thomas.* Minneapolis, MN: Fortress Press, 2002.

Schweitzer, Albert. *The Quest of the Historical Jesus: A Critical Study of Its Progress From Reimarus to Wrede.* London, UK: Adam and Charles Black, 1910.

Seabrook, Lochlainn. *The Goddess Dictionary of Words and Phrases: Introducing a New Core Vocabulary for the Women's Spirituality Movement.* 1997. Franklin, TN: Sea Raven Press, 2010 ed.

——. *Britannia Rules: Goddess-Worship in Ancient Anglo-Celtic Society - An Academic Look at the United Kingdom's Matricentric Spiritual Past.* 1999. Franklin, TN: Sea Raven Press, 2010 ed.

——. *The Book of Kelle: An Introduction to Goddess-Worship and the Great Celtic Mother-Goddess Kelle, Original Blessed Lady of Ireland.* 1999. Franklin, TN: Sea Raven Press, 2010 ed.

——. *Christmas Before Christianity: How the Birthday of the "Sun" Became the Birthday of the "Son."* Franklin, TN: Sea Raven Press, 2010.

——. *Jesus and the Law of Attraction: The Bible-Based Guide to Creating Perfect Health, Wealth, and Happiness Following Christ's Simple Formula.* Franklin, TN: Sea Raven Press, 2013.

——. *The Bible and the Law of Attraction: 99 Teachings of Jesus, the Apostles, and the Prophets.* Franklin, TN: Sea Raven Press, 2013.

——. *Christ Is All and In All: Rediscovering Your Divine Nature and the Kingdom Within.* Franklin, TN: Sea Raven Press, 2014.

——. *The Way of Holiness: The Story of Religion and Myth From the Cave Bear Cult to Christianity.* Unpublished manuscript. Franklin, TN: Sea Raven Press.

Simms, P. Marion. *The Bible in America.* New York, NY: Wilson-Erickson, 1936.

Smith, Daniel A. *The Post-Mortem Vindication of Jesus in the Sayings Gospel Q.* London, UK: T and T Clark International, 2006.

Smith, William. *A Dictionary of the Bible.* 3 vols. London, UK: John Murray, 1863.

Spalding, Baird T. *Life and Teachings of the Masters of the Far East.* 5 vols. 1924. Marina del Rey, CA: DeVorss and Co., 1964 ed.

Staniforth, Maxwell (trans.). *Early Christian Writings: The Apostolic Fathers.* 1968. Harmondsworth, UK: Penguin, 1984 ed.

Stanley, Arthur Penrhyn. *Lectures on the History of the Jewish Church.* 2 vols. New

York, NY: Scribner, Armstrong, and Co., 1877.

Stott, John R. W. *The Cross of Christ*. Downers Grove, IL: InterVarsity Press, 1986.

Strauss, David Friedrich, Peter C. Hodgson, and George Eliot. *The Life of Jesus Critically Examined*. Philadelphia, PA: Fortress Press, 1972.

Streeter, Burnett Hillman. *The Four Gospels: A Study of Origins*. 1924. London, UK: Macmillan and Co., 1930 ed.

Sypherd, W. O. *The Literature of the English Bible*. New York, NY: Oxford University Press, 1938.

Szekely, Edmond Bordeaux. *The Essene Gospel of Peace* (Book 1). 1928. London, UK: International Biogenic Society, 1978 ed.

Taylor, Vincent. *The Formation of the Gospel Tradition*. London, UK: Macmillan and Co., 1935.

Theissen, Gerd. *The First Followers of Jesus: A Sociological Analysis of the Earliest Christianity*. London, UK: SCM Press, 1978.

Tödt, Heinz Eduard. *The Son of Man in the Synoptic Tradition*. London, UK: SCM Press, 1965.

Torrey, Charles Cutler. *Our Translated Gospels: Some of the Evidence*. New York, NY: Harper and Brothers, 1936.

Townsend, Rev. Mark. *Jesus Through Pagan Eyes: Bridging Neopagan Perspectives with a Progressive Vision of Christ*. Woodbury, MN: Llewellyn, 2012.

Underhill, Evelyn. *The Mystic Way: A Psychological Study in Christian Origins*. London, UK: J. M. Dent and Sons, 1913.

Wake, Archbishop (and other divines). *The Forbidden Books of the Original New Testament of Jesus Christ*. London, UK: E. Hancock and Co., 1863.

Walker, Barbara G. *The Woman's Encyclopedia of Myths and Secrets*. San Francisco, CA: Harper and Row, 1983.

Watts, Alan W. *Myth and Ritual in Christianity*. Boston, MA: Beacon Press, 1968.

Weigall, Arthur. *The Paganism in Our Christianity*. New York, NY: G. P. Putnam's Sons, 1928.

Weiss, Bernhard. *A Manual of Introduction to the New Testament*. 2 vols. London, UK: Hodder and Stoughton, 1879-1889.

Weisse, Christian Hermann. *Die Evangelische Geschichte: Kritisch und Philosophisch Bearbeitet*. Leipzig, Germany: Breitkopf und Härtel, 1838.

Wells, G. A. *The Historical Evidence For Jesus*. Buffalo, NY: Prometheus, 1988.

Westcott, Brooke Foss. *History of the Canon of the New Testament*. New York, NY: Macmillian 1896.

Wild, Laura H. *The Romance of the English Bible*. New York, NY: Doran, 1929.

INDEX

MEET THE AUTHOR

LOCHLAINN SEABROOK, winner of the prestigious Jefferson Davis Historical Gold Medal for his "masterpiece," *A Rebel Born: A Defense of Nathan Bedford Forrest*, is a historian, award-winning author, Civil War scholar, Bible scholar, and traditional Southern Agrarian of Scottish, English, Irish, Welsh, German, and Italian extraction. An encyclopedist, lexicographer, anthologist, musician, artist, graphic designer, genealogist, and photographer, as well as an award-winning poet, songwriter, and screenwriter, he has a forty year background in historical nonfiction writing and is a member of the Sons of Confederate Veterans, the Civil War Trust, and the National Grange.

Due to similarities in their writing styles, ideas, and literary works, Seabrook is often referred to as the "next SHELBY FOOTE," the "new JOSEPH CAMPBELL," the "Southern CHARLES FILLMORE," and the "American ROBERT GRAVES," the latter who is his cousin: prolific English writer, historian, mythographer, poet, and author of the classic tomes *The White Goddess* and *The Greek Myths*.

A cousin of KING JAMES (whose Medieval English translation of the Bible is still the world's most popular version), and a descendant of both the Grail King MEROVECH (Frankish founder of the Merovingian dynasty) and TIBERIUS CAESAR (emperor of Rome during the time of Jesus, Luke 3:1), Seabrook is the grandson of an Appalachian coal-mining family, a seventh-generation Kentuckian, co-chair of the Jent/Gent Family Committee (Kentucky), founder and director of the Blakeney Family Tree Project, and a board member of the Friends of Colonel Benjamin E. Caudill. Seabrook's literary works have been endorsed by leading authorities, museum curators, award-winning historians, bestselling authors, celebrities, noted scientists, TV show hosts, well respected educators, renown military artists, esteemed Southern organizations, and distinguished academicians from around the world.

(Illustration © Sea Raven Press)

As a writer Seabrook has authored forty popular adult books specializing in the following genres and topics: the American Civil War, pro-South studies, Confederate biographies, anthologies, and histories, genealogical monographs, theology, thealogy, spirituality, mythology, Jesus, the Bible, the Apocrypha, esoterica, the Law of Attraction, self-help, healing, health, anthropology, ghost stories, the paranormal, family histories, military encyclopedias, etymological dictionaries, ufology, social issues, comparative analysis of the origins of Christmas, and cross-cultural studies of the family and marriage.

Seabrook's eight children's books include a Southern children's guide to the Civil War, a biography of Nathan Bedford Forrest for teens, a dictionary of religion and myth, a rewriting of the King Arthur legend (which reinstates the original pre-Christian motifs), two bedtime stories for preschoolers, a naturalist's guidebook to owls, a worldwide look at the family, and an examination of the near-death experience.

Of blue-blooded Southern stock through his Kentucky, Tennessee, Virginia, West

Virginia, and North Carolina ancestors, he is a direct descendant of European royalty via his 6th great-grandfather, the EARL OF OXFORD, after which London's famous Harley Street is named. Among his celebrated male Celtic ancestors is ROBERT THE BRUCE, King of Scotland, Seabrook's 22nd great-grandfather. The 21st great-grandson of EDWARD I "LONGSHANKS" PLANTAGENET), King of England, Seabrook is a 13th-generation Southerner through his descent from the colonists of Jamestown, Virginia (1607), and the 17th great-grandson of Earl RICHARD WOODVILLE, the father of the Medieval English QUEEN ELIZABETH, depicted in the TV series *The White Queen.*

Seabrook is related to numerous Confederate icons and other 19th-Century luminaries, among them: ROBERT E. LEE, NATHAN BEDFORD FORREST, STONEWALL JACKSON, ALEXANDER H. STEPHENS, JESSE JAMES, JEB STUART, JOHN HUNT MORGAN, NATHANIEL F. CHEAIRS, EDMUND W. RUCKER, STATES RIGHTS GIST, RICHARD TAYLOR, JOHN S. MOSBY, JOHN B. WOMACK, PIERRE G. T. BEAUREGARD, JOHN BELL HOOD, THEODRICK "TOD" CARTER, ABRAM POINDEXTER MAURY, WILLIAM GILES HARDING, JOHN W. McGAVOCK, and MARY CHESNUT.

Born with music in his blood, Seabrook is an award-winning, multi-genre, BMI-Nashville songwriter and lyricist who has composed some 3,000 songs (250 albums), and whose original music has been heard on TV and radio worldwide. In 2012 his poignant ballad *That's My Girl*—recorded and produced by JOHN CARTER CASH (son of JOHNNY CASH and executive producer of the five-time Academy Award-winning film *Walk the Line*)—was selected for inclusion in the film *Cowgirls N' Angels*, starring BAILEE MADISON, JACKSON RATHBONE, and JAMES CROMWELL.

Also an acclaimed screenwriter, Seabrook's pro-South script *A Rebel Born* (based on the award-winning book of the same name) has been picked up by renowned filmmaker Christopher Forbes (of Forbes Film). The historically accurate movie project is now in pre-production, and promises to be the most talked about feature Civil War film ever produced: the story of Lincoln's War as seen through the eyes of the South.

A musician, producer, multi-instrumentalist, and renown performer—whose keyboard work has been variously compared to pianists from HARGUS ROBBINS and VINCE GUARALDI to ELTON JOHN and LEONARD BERNSTEIN—Seabrook has opened for groups such as the EARL SCRUGGS REVIEW, TED NUGENT, and BOB SEGER, and has performed privately for such public figures as PRESIDENT RONALD REAGAN, BURT REYNOLDS, and SENATOR EDWARD W. BROOKE.

Seabrook's cousins in the entertainment business include: JOHNNY CASH, ELVIS PRESLEY, BILLY RAY and MILEY CYRUS, PATTY LOVELESS, TIM McGRAW, LEE ANN WOMACK, DOLLY PARTON, PAT BOONE, NAOMI, WYNONNA, and ASHLEY JUDD, RICKY SKAGGS, THE SUNSHINE SISTERS, MARTHA CARSON, CHET ATKINS, REESE WITHERSPOON, ANDY GRIFFITH, TOM CRUISE, CINDY CRAWFORD, REBECCA GAYHEART, and ROBERT DUVALL.

Seabrook lives with his wife and family in historic Middle Tennessee.

If you enjoyed Mr. Seabrook's *Jesus and the Gospel of Q* you will be interested in his other popular Christian works:

JESUS AND THE LAW OF ATTRACTION
CHRIST IS ALL AND IN ALL
THE BIBLE AND THE LAW OF ATTRACTION
CHRISTMAS BEFORE CHRISTIANITY

Available from Sea Raven Press and wherever fine books are sold.

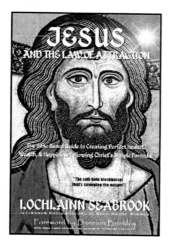
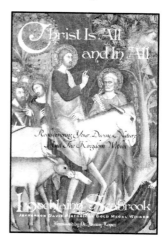

SeaRavenPress.com

CPSIA information can be obtained at www.ICGtesting.com
Printed in the USA
BVOW05s0014241014

372105BV00001B/92/P